DE
CRIM
CASEB

PETER JACKSON

Published by Cox & Jackson

ISBN 0 9532206 0 5

Printed by
The Ipswich Book Company Ltd,
The Drift,
Ipswich, Suffolk

Contents

*To my mother, who gave me my lifelong interest
in criminology*

Acknowledgements

Maureen Jackson, for her support and encouragement.
My stepdaughters, Nancy Ann and Emma Jane, and my personal assistant, Cheridah Sword, for all their interpreting during interviews and on the telephone.
Raymond Lee and John Hay of the British Deaf History Society for their support and contributions to several stories.
Arthur Dimmock and Simon Hesselberg for their support and assistance with two stories.
Tony Crompton for key information on stories around Tyne and Wear.
All those anonymous Deaf and Hearing contributors whom I interviewed.
Helen Krarup, of the University of Cambridge Institute of Criminology, and an unknown Danish law student who took it on as a project to research all criminal law cases relating to Deaf people.
Aynsley Sawyers, Librarian at Kilmarnock Library for assistance in research.
Various county constabularies for their time and assistance.
Robert Evans, Cataloguing Assistant, National Library of Wales, Aberystwyth.
And finally,
Ian Anstice, Paula Reilly-Cooper and Kathryn Arden of Winsford Library, Cheshire - for all of them, nothing was too much trouble in tracing and obtaining the information and records I needed.

1 :   Deaf Crime through the Ages - Introduction

Deaf criminology is a subject that has scarcely been covered by crime writers through the ages. Even well-known and popular criminology writers have tended to ignore crimes committed by Deaf people, and only television - always on the lookout for fresh drama documentaries - has occasionally strayed into this area.

Yet, it is a fascinating subject full of rich material, rarely unrecorded in crime magazines and books. This book was written to try and fill that gap, and to demonstrate to others the wealth of interest in the subject.

Part of this interest relates to the status of Deaf people coming up before the courts accused of crimes, and how the courts dealt with the cases before them.

Much of the time, courts preferred to hide behind legal precedent or definition and deal with Deaf accused accordingly, even if they were innocent. This meant that Deaf people who fell foul of the law were often treated much more harshly than others accused of similar crimes. They were often regarded as mentally or even morally defective if they were uneducated and could not speak, and classified alongside the insane and mentally-defective although many were able to go about their daily lives well enough communicating through sign language.

One of the most crucial aspects of early English law was that a person was required to respond *verbally* (i.e. that is, by speech) to the question whether he pled guilty or not guilty if arraigned for a criminal offence. If he could not do this, then it was found necessary to discover whether he stood mute by malice or by the visitation of God. If found to be by the visitation of God, the Deaf person was likely to be remanded to prison until such a time as he could speak, or His or Her Majesty's pleasure be known, which meant in some cases, for the rest of the unfortunate individual's natural life. This happened to a Deaf man accused of a felony during the reign of Edward III (1327-1377).

Almost a century later, one of England's leading justices, Sir Matthew Hale made a statement that :"A man who is *surdus et mutus a nativitate* (a deaf-mute) is in the presumption of the law an idiot, the rather because he hath no possibility to understand what is forbidden to be done or under what penalties. But if it appear that he hath the use of understanding, which many of that condition discover by signs to a great measure, he may be tried, and suffer judgement and execution, though great caution is to be used therein."

By this statement, any Deaf person who could communicate through sign language could be tried for his/her crime and suffer the consequences. In practice, this rarely - if ever - happened. (No Deaf person can be traced of having been legally executed before the case of Thomas Smallwood *aka* Brown in 1796, see page 21, and even in this case, it is evident that Brown could speak to some degree. He is the only known case of a deaf person to be legally executed in Britain).

Not until 1773 when the case of *Rex v. Thomas Jones* came up before the Old Bailey was Hale's statement taken literally, and judges started to accept that Deaf people could be tried, convicted and sentenced (in this case, to transportation). The same ruling was applied in the case of *Rex v. Elizabeth Steel* (1787), see page 17.

In the case of Jones, it would appear that his trial proceeded, and conviction resulted, because it was "proved" he was able to communicate through sign language with a woman friend named Fanny Lazarus, and understand her as well, and the woman Lazarus was accordingly summoned to the court to "interpret" for Jones.

In the case of Betty Steel, it was "proved" that she was an expert lipreader, and could follow proceedings.

Before those cases, Deaf people who fell foul of the law were sometimes dealt with **before** any court arraignment, sometimes by summary execution, sometimes by torture. In 1734, an unfortunate Deaf man named John Durrant was tortured to almost to death by thumbscrew in an effort to make him speak, and plead guilty to a charge of felony. When that failed, he was found guilty anyway and sentenced to transportation (see page 20).

A few years later, in 1745 when Bonnie Prince Charlie's Jacobean forces were quartered at Derby in their flight from the Duke of Cumberland's army, the Duke's soldiers arrested an unknown young Deaf man at Sutton Coldfield as a spy. When he could not answer the soldier's questions, he was summarily beheaded by the officer-in-charge of the party which threw the body into a ditch at Eachelhurst and carried the head in triumph on a sword into New Hall Farm, where the Duke's main party was quartered. There, it was thrown into an oak tree where it remained until the tree was chopped down in 1827, and the skull rolled out. Legend has it that sometimes towards dusk, the strange disembodied head of the Deaf youth is seen drifting across Wylde Green Road from the direction of New Shipton towards the ditch where his body was thrown.

The cases of Jones, Steel and Brown in the late 1700's are the last known cases where a Deaf person was tried, convicted and sentenced before the introduction of the Criminal Lunatics Act, 1800.

Commonly referred to by justices as "the stat. 39 & 40 Geo. 3, c.94, s.2", this Act (with subsequent amendments) laid down rules for dealing with Deaf persons arraigned for a crime which, as Mr. Justice (later Lord Chief Justice) Devlin was so succinctly to put it in the case of *Regina v. Roberts* (1953), see page 71, "What you are asking," Mr.Justice Devlin told the prosecution, "would mean that if I find the accused unfit to plead, I have to make an order under the Statute as a result of which he would be detained as a criminal lunatic and it would preclude any inquiry by the jury as to his guilt or not. In other words, it does not matter if he is guilty or not guilty, he is found to be a criminal lunatic anyway."

Two of the earliest cases where this statute applied to a Deaf person were *Rex. v. Dyson* (1831), see page 35, and *Rex. v. Pritchard* (1836). The latter is interesting in that the accused was on record of having had an education at the Deaf and Dumb Asylum in London, but it did not prevent him of being labelled a lunatic - a case perhaps that indicates the choice of the word 'asylum' as a name for this pioneering deaf school was unfortunate. The accused, William Pritchard, aged 28, came up for trial at Shropshire Assizes on 21st March 1836 accused of committing an unnatural sex act with an ass in the Abbey Foregate, Shrewsbury, and ordered to be kept in custody until His Majesty's pleasure be known, without having to go through a trial to prove whether he was guilty or not guilty of the alleged crime, although he was given the indictment to read and made a sign to the court that he was not guilty.

Thus, for well over a century and half, Deaf people coming up for trial for criminal offences risked, even if it was proved they had an education, being remanded to prison solely on the grounds that they were either unfit to plead guilty or not guilty, or on the grounds of the ruling made by Mr.Justice James Parke in the case of *Rex v.*

Dyson that as the Deaf accused did not have sufficient intelligence to comprehend the nature of the trial proceedings. "It is not enough," said Mr. Baron Alderson during the trial of William Pritchard, "that an accused may have a general capacity of communication on ordinary matters." In other words, even if an accused was fluent in sign language and could communicate through an interpreter, the accused was still held not to have sufficient intellect to understand what his or her trial was all about!

Not all Judges followed the dictum of Mr. Justice Parke or Mr. Baron Alderson literally. In the case of *Regina v. Daniel Whitfield* at Abingdon Assizes on 12th July 1850, where the accused was up for a case of attempted rape, Mr. Justice Vaughan-Williams was quite brusque in his findings.

A witness named Grimshaw testified : "The defendant is a farm labourer and understands his work very well."

Mr. Justice Vaughan-Williams :"That is not sufficient."

The next witness, a Mr. Judd, who stated he was the Governor of Abingdon Prison, said :"The defendant has perfect intellects by signs."

Mr. Justice Vaughan-Williams :"That is sufficient. Let the trial proceed."

So the trial of Daniel Whitfield proceeded, without an interpreter, and he was tried, convicted and sentenced to prison on a verdict of guilty of common assault with intent to rape. In this case, the accused clearly had no comprehension at all of what was happening in his trial without an interpreter!

It was not uncommon for Deaf accused to walk free from the court because no interpreter was found who could communicate the proceedings to them. This even happened in an assault case at West Riding magistrates at Bradford in 1904 when three accused were up for assault. Two were hearing men, and the third was Deaf man. The two hearing men were each fined £2 with costs, but the Deaf man was set free simply because there was no interpreter in court!

There was considerable protest in 1902 when a Deaf man named Frederick Emery appeared before Stafford Assizes on a charge of felony (to which he pleaded innocent) and was found to be non-sane under the provisions of the Criminal Lunatics Act and committed to Stafford Prison until His Majesty's pleasure be known. There was widespread belief that he would be found not guilty of the charge if only he was given the opportunity to prove it in court, and a writ of habeas corpus was lodged in 1909. In the Court of Criminal Appeal, the case of *Rex v. Governor of Stafford Prison, ex parte Emery*, the situation of wrongful imprisonment was fought, but the appeal court justices found that Frederick Emery had been correctly remanded to the prison under the provisions of the Act, and the appeal was dismissed. It is not known whether Frederick Emery was ever released from his wrongful confinement.

Mr. Justice Devlin's decision in *Regina v. Roberts* that it "cannot be our law that, by some formality of procedure, counsel for the defence should be prevented from (being able to submit evidence his client did not commit the crime) before the jury and so achieving for his client, if he can, a verdict of Not Guilty" was a landmark decision. It meant that Deaf people, especially those with no or little speech, could now fight to prove their innocence instead of being remanded to prison or institutions for the criminally insane indefinitely without the prospect of a fair trial.

Unfortunately, this did not always happen. There was one case in Birmingham in 1976 where a Deaf Black male was not tried because he was judged unfit to plead and remanded to a secure unit until 'Her Majesty's pleasure be known', but nowadays the treatment of Deaf suspects arrested by police in England, Wales and Northern Ireland are governed by the Codes of Practice issued under the provisions of the Police and Criminal Evidence Act, 1984, which should ensure that none of the circumstances surrounding the arrest of George Roberts in 1953 leading to his mockery of a trial should ever happen again.

Unhappily, in court, provisions for the engagement of sign language interpreters still remain inadequate despite the recommendations of the Royal Commission on Criminal Justice, 1993. This is mainly due to the scarcity of suitably qualified interpreters who have received training to interpret in court, but some lack of awareness of the needs of Deaf defendants (with or without the presence of other Deaf witnesses) by judges and counsel is also to blame in some cases, leading to the sometimes very expensive collapse of several trials during 1995 and 1996, see pages 178-179.

Attacks by learned judges and counsel on the integrity of sign language interpreters, as evidenced in the case of *Regina v. Ragu Shan* (1995) with the outburst by His Honour Judge Bruce Laughland, see page 178, were not helpful. It has to be remembered that the integrity of sign language interpreters is essential to prevent miscarriage of justices to Deaf people.

One such miscarriage of justice was prevented by the intervention of a sign language interpreter in the case of *Crown vs. Jean Campbell, alias Bruce* in Glasgow in 1817, see page 30. This case is included in this book simply because it is an important landmark in the history of Deaf criminology. It is the first recorded instance of a court-appointed sign language interpreter being used, notwithstanding the forced use of Fanny Lazarus in *Rex. v. Thomas Jones* in 1773, and it was only because of the stature and integrity of the person being used as sign language interpreter that Jean Campbell was properly acquitted of a charge of murder.

The stories in this book range from highway robbery and petty theft in the late 1700's to murder in the 1800's and 1900's. Included is also one unsolved murder of a deaf person.

The author does not feel that the fact there are more murders reported, and tried in court, during the 1990's is indicative of a rise of a new "breed" of Deaf criminals. It is simply that because of the Police and Criminal Evidence Act, and the Royal Commission on Criminal Justice, plus more open media reporting, there has been more prominence given to murders committed by Deaf people in the last decade of the 20th-Century. There were probably just as many murders by Deaf people in the 1900-1950 period - it is just that because Deaf accused were invariably classified as criminal lunatics and rarely had the opportunity of a full and fair trial, and/or thus were largely unreported - even by the Deaf media, it is much more difficult to trace the cases involved.

It is to be hoped that the reader will enjoy the stories that follow.

TRANSPORTATION

In the last half of the 18th Century, the prisons throughout England became so overcrowded due to a number of reasons.   Firstly, because of the Industrial Revolution, many people left the countryside and settled into cities and towns where there was hope of work to be obtained. This was true of those people who had been evicted from their homes to make way for the growth of the industrial revolution.

Not everybody, however, was able to obtain such work and to survive, many had to resort to petty crime.   The theft of personal property such as clothes or jewellery for the ease of which they could be resold for money became so common that between 1760 and 1810, over sixty crimes against theft of property, including petty theft, became capital crimes - that is, crimes which were punishable by death by hanging.   It proved impossible, however, to hang people faster than the rate at which they were being arrested and tried, so alternative methods of punishment had to be sought.   One such punishment was transportation to British colonies overseas which had started in 1614 with America being a favourite destination, though other colonies like Canada, the West Indies and Honduras were also used.

In London, Newgate prison was periodically 'cleared' of convicts who were needed to work in the American colonies of Maryland and Virginia.

In 1774, a Deaf man named Thomas Jones was transported to America after being convicted at the Old Bailey in December 1773 for burglary, the offence being the theft of five guineas from the dwelling house of John

Goldwell. It was found by the court that although Jones was 'mute by the visitation of God', he was well able to communicate through sign language and understand what was being said to him through a woman named Fanny Lazarus who lived with Jones, and was sworn to interpret for him by Mr. Justice Blackwell. It is not known what happened to Thomas Jones after he arrived in America as one of a batch of convicts making up the Middlesex Bond in either of the brigs *Thornton* or the *Green Garland*. These were two of the last ships to reach America before the start of American War of Independence, and records for the Middlesex Bond batch of prisoners are incomplete.

The American War of Independence of 1776 put a stop to all transportation of criminals to the newly-founded United States, and with Canada and the other colonies in the Americas no longer willing to accept convicts, a new destination for the transportation of convicts had to be found. The newly-discovered continent of Australia fitted this gap admirably. The problem was that Australia was on the other side of the world, and it took time to gather together the ships and the prisoners to be transported, and start up the penal colonies, and it was May 1787 before the convoy of ships known as the First Fleet sailed to Australia.

In the period between the sailing of the First Fleet, and the gathering of ships and convicts for the Second Fleet due to sail in 1789, it became urgent that the female prison population in England should be reduced, and one single ship, the *Lady Juliana*, was chartered to transport over 200 women convicts to New South Wales, sailing in July 1789, and arriving in Australia in June 1790, a voyage of eleven months which took in stops at Tenerife, Rio de Janiero (Brazil) and Table Bay (South Africa). On the long voyage, five women convicts died, but the rest arrived fit and healthy due in no small measure to the kindness of the captain and the crew. These women were more fortunate than the 1000 or more convicts that were carried by the Second Fleet that finally sailed in January 1790, arriving in New South Wales in July 1790.

The Second Fleet became notorious as the Death Fleet because the transports were experienced slave traders who were not inclined to treat the convicts with any degree of kindness with the result that by the time the ships arrived in Australia, well over a quarter of the convicts had died on the voyage and the rest were so ill that a severe strain was placed on the struggling penal colony.

Among the women transported on the *Lady Juliana* was a Deaf woman named Elizabeth Steel who became the first Deaf person to colonise Australia.

Elizabeth Steel, otherwise known as Betty Steel, was born in London in 1764 to a John and Sarah Steel, who had five other children though three died at childbirth. Elizabeth Steel's mother herself died in giving birth to her sixth child, a boy named James when the girl was only nine years old, and thereafter it was a tough life for her father and the three children in the slums of London around Smithfield Market and Fleet Street.

To survive and feed her younger brothers, Elizabeth Steel did anything she could to obtain food, resorting to petty theft and pickpocketing, and as she became older, she became a prostitute who was not above robbing her customers for any money or jewellery that they had, and this was to be her downfall.

One winter's night in January 1787, Elizabeth Steel was in the company of another prostitute when they met up with two men, a John Mills and a George Childs (himself a Deaf man), in a public house near Holborn in London and arranged separately to go upstairs to rooms for the purpose of having sex.

Shortly afterwards, there was a commotion and George Childs was observed staggering out of a room with his mouth bleeding. Of Elizabeth Steel, there was no sign. He alleged that he had been violently assaulted by the woman and his expensive watch had been taken from him.

Perhaps it had been a mistake to rob another Deaf person like George Childs because many Deaf people would know each other, and only an hour later the same night, 22nd January, Elizabeth Steel was spotted in another of her haunts and identified to a night-watchman by George Childs. Of the watch, there was no sign, and the Deaf woman could not say where it was. She was arrested and indicted the same night, and held in Clerkenwell Gaol for about a month before being transferred to the dreaded Newgate Prison where she remained until she appeared in court on 23rd May 1787 for the purpose of determining if she was able to plead because of her deafness, as was the custom at that time. She was found to be 'mute due the visitation of God' following similar custom, and sent to trial which took place on October 1787 at the Old Bailey.

Again, evidence was heard to determine her deafness, as there was some scepticism as to whether she was actually Deaf. Evidence was given that although she could speak to some degree and could lip-read sometimes, most people were convinced she was Deaf, and she was found, once again, to be 'mute due to the visitation of God.' Having settled upon this issue, the court then heard evidence of the theft of the watch from George Childs and of the assault upon him.

"She trust her hand into my breeches pocket where I had a shilling and two sixpences," said Childs. "There was a struggle, then she snatched my watch, ran out of the room and ran off, out of another door."

Childs stated that together with his friend John Mills, he had searched for 'Betty' and had seen her an hour later, but she did not have the watch any longer.

"Did you ask her where your watch was?" asked the judge.

"Yes."

"What did she say to you?"

"Nothing at all."

The jury returned a verdict of guilty against Elizabeth Steel, and she was sentenced to "transportation for seven years", and returned to Newgate Prison to await her fate, spending fifteen months there before being transferred to the *Lady Juliana* when that ship was at anchor in Greenwich.

Elizabeth Steel never returned to London from Australia. She did not even spend most of her time in Australia, but on Norfolk Island out in the Pacific Ocean to which she had been transferred in September 1790. She was to remain on Norfolk Island until her release from her sentence in 1794 when she married another ex-convict, James Mackey, who had become a soldier.

They both had lived together on a plot of land similar to many others which were allocated to convicts to cultivate and grow crops, and both returned, separately on different ships, to New South Wales where they had a small wooden house on a plot of land. They were only to be free together for a bare seven months, before Elizabeth died on 7th June 1795 old before her time at 31 years of age, worn by the privations she had suffered as a convict. It is also possible that she never recovered from the flogging she had received while on Norfolk Island when she had received the full fifty lashes.

Apart from Thomas Jones and John Durrant (who was transported to Maryland, U.S.A. in April 1734 in the brig *Patapsco Merchant* under the command of Darby Lux), it is not known if any other Deaf person was ever sentenced to transportation, whether to the Americas prior to 1776, or to Australia after Elizabeth Steel. Although there is a complete record of all convicts sentenced and transported, these lists do not tell us whether the person being transported was Deaf.

Postscript : Elizabeth Steel's story is known only because her gravestone was discovered in 1991 underneath a floor in Sydney Town Hall which was undergoing alterations at the time. The discovery caused newspapers to speculate about the remains found, and some research was undertaken by interested parties.

3 : 1796 : Cheshire

THE HIGHWAYMAN

"Stand and deliver!"
Those words struck terror in everyone who used the old highways and turnpikes in the 18th Century, when travelling posed great risk from robbers working the routes, either singly or in bands. The words also bring with them romantic images of Dick Turpin and his faithful horse, Bess.

There was nothing romantic about highway robbery, however, in the final decade of the 18th Century when the General Post Office's mail delivery system was being badly disrupted by bands of highway robbers, or highwaymen as they were called, and the penalties for being caught were very severe.

Since 1635, when Charles I introduced the system of delivering letters by horseback, mostly with local inns acting as collection points, postal services throughout Britain had developed into a vital service.

The appointment of John Palmer in October 1786 as Comptroller General of Postal Revenue saw many changes being made in the way the Royal Mail was being delivered through switching many postal routes from horseback delivery to fast, well-guarded stagecoach delivery. But implementation of the changes was slow, especially in rural areas and by the beginning of 1796, postal delivery routes along the turnpike roads in Cheshire were still being done by horseback, usually at night.

The horseback delivery riders were known as post-boys, although many of them were in fact not boys at all, but older men, but be they a boy or an older man, very few were able to resist the highwaymen determined to rob through the use of force the mail they carried for any valuables.

About 8.30 p.m. on Monday 18th January 1796, post-boy Peter Yoxall, aged 15, was carrying the Warrington to Chester mail and riding fast over Dunham Hill where about three-quarters of a mile on the Chester side of the hill, he came upon two men riding more slowly ahead of him. As he tried to pass between them, shouting, "Give way for the mail!", the two men turned their horses into him, blocking his path, and with one of them brandishing a small, bright pistol pushed under his nose, forced him to get off his horse, and led him into a nearby field.

Although the two highwaymen were both masked, it was a bright moonlit night and young Yoxall saw enough to be able to describe something of his attackers. He was also able to give his employers, the General Post Office, and the Constables an important clue when he described the robbery to them afterwards.

As the shorter man searched through the mailbags looking for bills and cash, leaving mail bound for Warrington and Manchester strewn about the field, the taller man started to tie him up roughly using coat straps.

"Hey!", Yoxall protested, "this is too tight!"

However, the taller highwayman did not understand him and continued to tie him up. As it turned out later, he was Deaf!

After the two robbers had left, with two bills of £150 and £8, and £1 in cash and three leather bags containing three shillings taken from the mail-bags, leaving Yoxall hoodwinked and fastened to a tree, the young post-boy struggled free of his shackles after one hour and half, and made his way to the parish constable at nearby Mickle Trafford.

From enquiries made by the General Post Office and the parish constable in the locality, information was received that two men had been seen at nearby Bridge Trafford eating lunch and having drinks at the Nag's Head Inn. After lunch, one of the men had taken his horse to the local blacksmith and requested that his mare be re-shod. He rather unwisely asked for the mare's forefeet to be fitted with double-channelled shoes, a distinctive thread pattern which would later leave clearly identifiable tracks at the scene of the robbery.

The same two men were seen later that afternoon by a person in the next village, Tarvin, asking two other people for directions, and again rather foolishly, they galloped past a gatekeeper at his toll-box without paying the toll fee. All four people would later give evidence at the two men's trial.

The descriptions circulated by the General Post Office stated that one of the men was aged between 18 and 20, five foot four or five inches in height, the other being between 25 and 30 years of age, five foot seven or eight inches tall. The taller man was said to be pitted with smallpox on his face. The clothes the men wore were meticulously described, and could only have come from descriptions furnished by witnesses who had seen them throughout the day, for it had been too dark for Peter Yoxall to see them.

While the General Post Office was circulating their descriptions, the two men were travelling fast to Birmingham where they hoped to rob another post-boy. After brief stops at Tarporley, Nantwich, and Woore, they arrived at Wolverhampton on the afternoon of the 20th January. Forced by the condition of their horses to stop travelling by horseback, they arranged with someone for them to be delivered later in Birmingham after the horses had recovered from their journey, and caught the post-chaise (a form of stagecoach) to Birmingham, arriving there late that night.

Their fast journey, the way they had forced the pace of their horses, the condition of the horses themselves on arrival at Wolverhampton did not escape notice. Too many people saw and remembered them.

When the news of the Dunham Hill robbery also travelled fast, people put two and two together and identified the two men. A reward of £200, a very large sum of money for the late 18th Century, was also a very good reason for so many people coming forward to point the way the robbers had gone.

By the time the two men had arrived in Birmingham, they had tentatively been identified as James Price, aged 20, of Manchester, who was a known pickpocket, and Thomas Brown, aged 26, of Thornton-le-Moors, Cheshire. Brown was known to be deaf!

When neither man could be found at their homes or lodgings, although Brown's wife and child were still at home, suspicion gave way to certainty that these were the two highway robbers.

Thomas Brown was born Thomas Smallwood in Willenhall, a village near Wolverhampton in Staffordshire. It is not known why he changed his name to Brown, but one reason may be that he had an uncle to whom he was apprenticed as a sawyer. The uncle's name was Brown.

How deaf Thomas Brown was cannot be ascertained but he could evidently make himself understood through speech and some gestures. He had become deaf through smallpox, not an uncommon occurrence in those times.

By the time he was 20, Brown had become a travelling hawker of Manchester and Birmingham goods, touring the North and the Midlands in a caravan, becoming fairly well-known as a trader because of his deafness and his shrewdness in transactions. He was almost always accompanied by his wife and child in the caravan.

By 1790, Brown was buying and selling horses legally, and met a man called John Hewitt, and fell in love with Hewitt's stepsister, and set out to woo her. After his marriage to her, he moved with her in 1794 to live in the parish of Over in Winsford where he had a child by her.

For a period of time, Brown lived with his wife and child in Royston, Hertfordshire where he kept a gig and two stablemen, and was well-respected in the community until he was arrested at Weyhill Fair for robbing a Quaker. He got out of this and returned to Cheshire where he took up with Hewitt.

John Hewitt was a member of a gang of horsethieves operating throughout Lancashire, Cheshire and Shropshire, and Brown began a partnership with him stealing and selling horses. From 1793 to 1795, the pair prospered so well as horsethieves and horse traders that they had to employ two stablehands and successfully building up a reputation in the community for the quality of their horses

But in late 1795, Brown's world crashed when he and Hewitt were arrested for horsestealing. Hewitt was taken to Lancaster Gaol for trail but Brown managed to buy his release which left him poor, and unable to provide for his family at Christmas.

James Price had a lucky escape in Liverpool in November 1795 when his partner James Berry tried to sell a money order picked from someone's pocket and was caught. Price was on watch outside at the time and managed to get away. Berry ended up in Lancaster Gaol where he was put in with Hewitt. Both men were put on trial at the

April assizes in Lancaster where they were found guilty and executed on the same day by hanging.

Thus when Brown and Price met in Birmingham at Christmas 1795, they had lost their partners in crime, and were poor. They already knew each other from previous meetings at livestock fairs in Manchester and other northern towns, and therefore decided to go into partnership.

But it was not at pickpocketing or horsestealing that Brown and Price decided to recover their fortunes - they decided to try their hand at highway robbery and become highwaymen!

The robbery of post-boy Peter Yoxall was their very first try at robbing the mails, and as seen, it was doomed to failure from the start because the two men made so many mistakes.

Brown, because of his deafness and horse dealing, was too well-known in Cheshire and surrounding districts, and Price was too young and inexperienced to plan anything properly. In addition, their wild ride through Cheshire and Staffordshire on worn-out horses drew too much attention to them.

In Wolverhampton, Brown, as an experienced horse trader, had recognised that their horses could do no more so he had them taken to a friend he had known from the time he had lived in Willenhall. The friend was working as a carter, and promised to bring the horses to a stables in Livesey Street, Birmingham when the horses had recovered from their journey, and Brown would collect them from there.

However, the reward of £200 posted for the capture of the two highwaymen proved to be too tempting, and overcoming loyalty to his childhood friend, the carter went together with his brother to see Constable Tart of Aston and after eliciting a promise from him they would get the reward, they tipped the constable off as to the whereabouts of the two wanted men.

The tip-off took Constable Tart, together with his son, to a public house near Birmingham where they found Price and Brown playing cards with two other men. Price and Brown were arrested without much struggle after being surprised. Although Price had three loaded pistols on him, Brown who had vowed never to be captured had left his own pistols in his bedroom!

"...which was lucky for Tart otherwise I would have shot him.."

Between January 22nd and January 26th, both men were identified by the landlord of the Nag's Head as the two men who had ate lunch and drank in his inn, and by the blacksmith who had a horse's (Brown's) shoes fitted with such distinctive patterns on the afternoon of the robbery that they were to be so easily identifiable at the scene of the robbery. They were then held in custody in the parish constable's house before making the journey in chains to Chester Gaol.

The trial of Price and Brown began on 6th April 1796 at Chester Assizes before Mr.Justice Burton. Over 20 people who had witnessed the prisoners' movements on the day of the mail robbery, and their hectic and furious ride from Dunham Hill to Wolverhampton gave evidence to the jury over a period of three days.

On 9th April, both men were in court when the jury returned from their deliberations and announced their verdicts. It was in fact a foregone conclusion in face of the overwhelming evidence that the only possible verdicts could be guilty, and Mr.Justice Burton then sentenced them to death by public hanging.

It was said of Thomas Brown at his trial that no man had apparently kept better company, that he had always put up in the best inns and paid his way regularly. He was always ready to assist persons in distress and was never guilty of the least cruelty. However, his involvement with horse-stealers and receivers of stolen horses in various counties led to his ruin.

After a brief stay in Chester Gaol, the two reckless highwaymen were publicly executed on Saturday 30th April 1796 at Boughton, Chester on a spot overlooking the River Dee. They were hanged side by side, and afterwards their bodies were taken down and transported to Trafford Green, a spot on the Warrington to Chester road about two miles from where the robbery had taken place.

There, the two bodies were suspended side by side on a gibbet and left to rot there for many years as a warning to any other person who might be foolish enough to think about robbing the mails.

In 1820, the piece of land at Trafford Green where the rotting remains of the gibbet stood was enclosed, and the gibbet and its occupants were removed. It was said that a robin's nest was found inside Price's skull. That piece of land is still known on maps locally as Gibbet Field.

Although the mail stagecoach routes expanded rapidly throughout the country in the early 1800's, Cheshire's rural postal delivery routes still used post-boys up to 1837 when they were replaced by the new railway routes. The Chester to Northwich route was the last to stop using post-boys to carry the mails.

Although it is difficult to prove, it seems likely that Thomas Brown was the last Deaf Highwayman, and because no other Deaf person has ever been known to have received the death penalty, may have been the only Deaf person to be hanged and gibbeted.

In his cell, Brown left behind some writing on the wall above his bed, showing a drawing of a coffin and the following lines:

Behold the corpse within the coffin lies,
With stretch'd out limbs, and closed eyes;
But ah! poor Brown! no coffin thou shalt have,
Nor yet a shroud, nor yea a peaceful grave.
Prisoners all a warning by me take,
Repent in time, before it be too late;
Repent in time, leave off your thieving ways;
Then you shall all see happier days.

4 :   1817 : Glasgow, Scotland

THE DROWNED BABY

When one April night in 1817 a baker's delivery boy heard a cry followed by a splash in the River Clyde flowing under Glasgow's old Saltmarket bridge, and found a dishevelled and drunken woman with her hands around the head of a little boy, the cry of "Wilful Murder!" that went up was to have far-reaching consequences in the history of Deaf people and the Law.

Since Solon created the ancient Greek laws in Athens in 591 BC, which were used by the Romans to form the basis of their Justinian Code, deaf people were regarded as imbeciles and incapable of conducting their affairs. They were forbidden to possess any kind of property, allowed no redress or the means to seek it and were not permitted to give any form evidence whether for or against in any court or tribunal. In English law, the deaf person had no legal status up to the time of Henry III when legislature condescended to notice him but only as the sad 'victim of frailty and the power of heavenly wrath.' For any deaf person to fall into the clutches of the law, the consequences could be severe, often leading to torture in attempts to prove that he or she really could not speak, as evidenced in the opening chapter.

By the early 19th Century, the laws had relaxed a little to recognise the status of *educated* deaf people who were permitted to possess property, to sue and be sued, and to manage their affairs. Furthermore, education for deaf children was largely still in its infancy and although there had been a school for deaf children in Edinburgh since 1760, there was still no legal provision for state education of Deaf children.

But the sworn testimony of any deaf person accused of a crime, particularly one classified in those days as a deaf-mute, meaning that he or she could neither hear or speak, had yet to be tested in a criminal law court although there was an earlier case, *Rex v. Bartlett [1786]* where the main witness against an accused was a deaf person named Rushton who was uneducated and unable to speak, but the court - possibly anxious to convict the accused - accepted his testimony as interpreted by his sister who was alleged to be able to communicate with the witness.

So, when Jean Campbell *alias* Bruce was accused of throwing over the Saltmarket bridge her three year-old child and murdering it by drowning, it became crucial for the Judges and the Advocates to determine to what extent they could accept her testimony, and in particular her understanding of what was right and what was wrong, and that if she did wrong wilfully, she would be punished for the crime. It was also important to determine if she had the power of communicating her thoughts.

Jean Campbell, in 1817, was an uneducated deaf-mute who could only write the initials of her name in reverse order, e.g.. C.J. She was an unmarried woman who had three children by different men, one of whom she had been living with as a common-law husband up to a few days before the alleged murder. He had then taken off the ring he had given to her which she had worn on her finger in the fashion of a married woman, and had left home to live with another woman to whom he had given Jean Campbell's ring.

Upset by this desertion of her man, Campbell had wandered through several alehouses in Glasgow in a fit of depression, accompanied by two of her children. During the evening she had drank 8 glasses of whisky which had left her intoxicated. While crossing the old Saltmarket

31

bridge, she had suddenly wondered if she still had with her the money which she carried with her in her breast purse, and had rested the youngest child whom she had been carrying on her back, covered by her petticoat and a duffel cloak, on the parapet of the bridge, the child being asleep. Holding him with one hand while she used the other to search through her clothing for her money, the child slipped from her grasp and fell into the river below where it drowned.

However, unable to communicate and because of the way she had her hands round the head of the other, older child, she was arrested and put into the gaol in Glasgow to await trial for the murder of her baby.

Whilst she was in gaol awaiting trial, she was visited by Robert Kinniburgh, who was headmaster of the Institution of the Deaf and Dumb in Edinburgh. Because of his knowledge of sign language, Kinniburgh had been engaged by the courts to interpret the story of Jean Campbell. He was accompanied on one occasion by a Dr.William Farquharson, a physician appointed by the court, and a Mr.Wood, the Auditor of Excise, who were both to testify at a pre-trial hearing called by the High Court of Justiciary in Glasgow on 17th July 1817 that they had formed the opinion that although the accused did not understand the nature and consequences of pleading guilty or not guilty, she did understand the distinction between right and wrong and that if she did wilfully throw the child into the river, she was liable to punishment, and that she was currently imprisoned on account of causing the death of her child.

Robert Kinniburgh, in his evidence to the court, stated that in his opinion the prisoner, although uneducated, was capable of conveying her thoughts by signs and facial expression. He said that Jean Campbell had been indignant at the imputation that she had wilfully caused the death of her child, which she said was a simple accident. He had formed this opinion because she had showed she understood the notion of marriage, although he doubted she was legally married herself, and that she had understood the criminality of theft and right from wrong.

Two other witnesses who were called, the baker's boy and a man named Sibbault who was employed as the keeper of the tollbooth on Saltmarket bridge were also called to give evidence in the hearing.

The baker's boy stated that he had heard the accused cry out, and the splash as the child hit the water, and that she had communicated to him by signs that the child had fallen off her back into the water.

Sibbault, the tollbooth keeper, stated that he had known Jean Campbell for some time and understood a little of her sign language, that generally she conducted herself rationally but had sometimes been distressed and intoxicated, and had sometimes seen her weep. On the night of the alleged murder, she had been very distressed and had communicated to him the uneasiness of her mind that something had fallen from her back into the river.

The Court decided that Jean Campbell was capable of standing trial, and accordingly committed her to the next circuit, to be held in Glasgow on 24th September 1817, instructing counsel on both sides to prepare the relevant evidence and depositions.

She pleaded not guilty in sign language through Robert Kinniburgh as interpreter, and at the wish of the court, proceeded communicate through the interpreter to the court what had happened, that she had stopped to place the child on the parapet while she searched for her money, and that she had lost hold of her child, and that it was an accident, not deliberate.

Mr.Kinniburgh testified that the story Jean Campbell had told through him to the court was the same as she had told to him when he visited her in prison prior to the trial.

The Court then found that there was no case to answer, and Jean Campbell was acquitted.

Although this case did not result in any conviction, it was of very significant and important interest for two reasons. One was that it raised a legal ruling as to whether the untaught deaf people who could not speak could be held responsible for their crimes, and set a precedent that overturned centuries of law which did not permit deaf persons to be able to give evidence in a court of law or a tribunal.

The second point of considerable interest is that the case of the *Crown vs. Jean Campbell* alias *Bruce* provided the first occasion anywhere in the world where a person was **appointed** by a court to assist in the questioning of, and providing answers from, a deaf person and of having that testimony accepted in the court, whereas in the past (as in *The King v. Thomas Jones*, see chapter I, or in *Rex v. Bartlett*, see above) anyone who could more or less allegedly communicate with a Deaf witness was pressed into service in court as a so-called interpreter.

AN UNFORTUNATE PREGNANCY

In the early nineteenth century, Ecclesfield was a small village on the outskirts of Sheffield, dominated by cotton treadmills. As with most villages of its kind, it was a close-knit community where most people knew each other, even if they did not speak to each other. Consequently, if you were Deaf and communicated in sign language, you were bound to get noticed.

Esther Dyson did get noticed, not just because she was Deaf, but also because she was an attractive woman of approximately 21 years.

Born in 1808 or 1809 (the date is uncertain but parish records show she was baptised on 30 April 1809), she was the third surviving child of Isaac and Eliza Dyson. The other children were William, (born in 1804) who was also Deaf, and Sarah (born in 1806), who was hearing.

Esther lived with her brother William in a two-up, two-down cottage, and communicated with each other in sign language, and with another Deaf youth in the village, the son of mill-owner Thomas Yeardley who ran the Ecclesfield Mill. Because of his own Deaf child, Yeardley gave employment to William and Esther Dyson in his mill. He also obtained some books on the education of deaf people which included pictures of the alphabet and some signs. Yeardley encouraged William and Esther to have private lessons with his son, and engaged a local, educated midwife Ann Briggs for a 12-month period of tuition for all three. At the end of this period, Ann Briggs could communicate with them in sign language, and the Dysons had received a sort of basic education. It is not known what or which books they were that were being used as aids in the education of three young Deaf people in the village of Ecclesfield, but it seems that this education served to enable young Yeardley, William and Esther Dyson to be regarded as shrewd and intelligent persons, notwithstanding their use of sign language. Certainly, both William and Esther Dyson could write their own names, which was more than could be said for their next door neighbours, a Ellen Greaves and her husband Thomas, a filecutter in another mill.

Although illiterate, Ellen Greaves did however pick up enough use of sign language to be able to communicate with her Deaf neighbours, as did another neighbour named Hannah Butcher. It seemed that Esther Dyson was not above teaching her hearing neighbours some sign language.

Living next door as she did, Ellen Greaves was always calling on the Dysons and when in the early summer of 1830, Ellen gave birth to a baby girl, one of the first persons she showed it to was her friend Esther Dyson. She also teased Esther about her own swelling belly, saying she would be soon with child too and could be a playmate of her baby girl.

But this was 1830 when to be an unmarried mother and being a bastard child carried great stigma, so Esther Dyson reacted angrily and vigorously denied that she was pregnant.

The more she was challenged about her pregnancy, not only by Ellen Greaves but also by other neighbours like Hannah Butcher, the angrier Esther became in her denials, and she started to shun her neighbours, becoming a bit of a recluse although she found it difficult to avoid seeing Ellen Greaves, who on Wednesday 22nd September, signed to Esther that she would soon be nursing and suckling a child and that she had better get some baby linen and clothes in. Esther made a foul face and denied that she was with child, saying that she had took some stuff for a bad throat and this had caused her stomach to swell.

When next seen, it was Friday the 24th September around noon, and Esther Dyson was standing in the front doorway of her house, looking very big in the family way. When she spotted Ellen Greaves looking at her, Esther turned and went inside her house, fastening the front door shut preventing entry and drawing together all the curtains.

At about 9 o'clock the following morning, Ellen Greaves noticed the front door was open, and taking the opportunity, she went inside and found Esther Dyson on her knees scrubbing the floor. She seemed to have lost weight, had a flannel tied round her neck and appeared pale and languid. The Deaf girl was not pleased to see her neighbour, and tried to get her out of the house, signing that she had vomited up a large substance into the sink.

After Esther, assisted by her brother William, had pushed their neighbour out of the house, they fastened the door shut to prevent further entry, and drew together all the curtains. Ellen Greaves went round to Hannah Butcher and told her that Esther had given birth to a child, and the two women made numerous attempts to gain entry to the Dyson house throughout the day, without success - the door being kept firmly shut in their faces.

For the rest of that Saturday, the door remained firmly shut and the news soon spread through the small village of Ecclesfield that "the Dumb Girl" had given birth to a bastard child.

The next day, at around 3 p.m.., William Dyson opened the door in response to Ellen Greaves' hammering and signed to her that his sister was in bed very sick, and refused to let her go up.

Mrs.Greaves refused to give up, and went to get Hannah Butcher, returning to the Dyson house an hour later, when they were let inside by William Dyson. As they were being let inside, they saw Esther Dyson coming down the stairs with a pillow in her hand. She used the pillow to sit on, and "appeared to be very poorly."

"Go make tea for her." Ellen Greaves signed to William Dyson, as Hannah Butcher laid her hands on his sister, feeling her bosom and stomach. Esther pushed the hands away weakly.

The two neighbour women stayed about an hour, and although they had no doubt at all Esther Dyson had delivered a child, probably in the afternoon or evening of the previous day, the Deaf girl continued to insist that she was sick through throwing up a large substance.

Feeling concerned, they went to see a James Hinderson immediately they left the Dyson house, and poured out their worries to him about the Dysons. As Hinderson was a person of some authority, being an Overlooker of the Ecclesfield Treadmill and who was directly responsible for the employment of William and Esther Dyson at the Mill, he also knew a bit of sign language having employed the Dysons for 11 years. Having heard what the women had to say, he decided to go and see the Dysons himself.

Hinderson called at the Dyson house at about 7 p.m. the Sunday evening, and asked William Dyson for the keys to his room, also Esther Dyson's room.

There was nothing suspicious in the brother's room, but Hinderson found blood on the floor under the bed in Esther's room which had been partly wiped up. There was also blood against the wall underneath the chamber window, and on the window sill itself. More blood was found on the opposite wall, and in a hand box, Hinderson found two aprons and a skirt stained with blood. Several times whilst Hinderson was in the room, Esther Dyson signed to him to get out and go downstairs - instructions which he ignored.

Having satisfied himself that Esther Dyson had indeed probably given birth, and that something had gone wrong, he went to see the vestry clerk, James Machin who returned to the Dyson house with Hinderson to see for himself.

Together, they went to see the village constable, William Shaw and reported their suspicions to him.

By then, many rumours had been going round the village about Esther Dyson and her bastard child, and as a result of two people coming forward with information, the constable went first thing the next morning as soon as it was daylight to search a place called the Cotton Mill Dam, accompanied by James Machin. After a thorough search, Shaw found two green cloth bundles. One bundle contained the body of a fully-grown, new born baby girl - minus its head! The other bundle contained the head itself. The pieces of green cloth were identified as part of the cover of a sofa belonging to William Dyson.

Both William and Esther Dyson were arrested for the murder of the newly-born child, and brought to Ecclesfield workhouse to view the little body.

Confronted with the body of her newly-delivered daughter, Esther Dyson admitted it was hers but insisted first in response to questioning by James Hinderson, then by her former teacher, the midwife Ann Briggs, that the baby had come out feet first, and she had pulled the feet during the delivery to get the baby out, and the head had come off.

Ann Briggs challenged Esther on this statement, saying that it was not possible for a baby's head to be torn off the way she had described, and that the only way it could have been separated from its body was to have been cut off. This was strongly denied by the accused girl.

Further questioning came from Sarah Ingham, the governess of the workhouse to which the baby had been taken, who produced a knife and signed to Esther how the baby's head had been removed. Again, this accusation was denied. Mrs.Ingham also examined Esther Dyson's body, and found that her breasts were heavy with milk, and there were signs of recently having given birth.

In William Dyson's presence, Esther was asked what he had to do with the birth, and subsequent murder. Esther insisted her brother had nothing to do with the death, so William Dyson was released. Before he left the workhouse, he asked his sister by signs why she had thrown the child into the water of the dam. She refuted that, signing that she had merely laid it down on the bank of the dam.

Esther Dyson was held in the workhouse until the inquest took place on Thursday 30th September before the District Coroner, Mr.B.Badger, in the Black Bull Inn, Ecclesfield, where the body and head of the child were viewed.

The inquest took the best part of twelve hours to hear evidence from a number of people. A key part of the inquest, as was the custom in those days, was to determine whether Esther Dyson had the capacity of understanding the nature of the alleged crime. The chief witnesses were Ellen Greaves, Esther's former friend and next door neighbour, Ann Briggs, her former tutor and James Hinderson.

Mrs.Greaves detailed how she had consistently challenged the accused about her pregnancy, and described the events of the previous Friday and Saturday when the alleged birth had taken place, and how she had attempted without success to gain access to the Dyson house to check upon Esther. She described the difference in Esther Dyson's appearance between Friday the 24th, and the next morning at 9 o'clock, and how sick and unwell the Deaf girl had been. She gave it as her considered opinion from the altered appearance that a child had been born between those sightings.

Asked by the Coroner as to the intellectual capacity of Esther Dyson, Mrs. Greaves stated that "she has sufficient knowledge in my opinion to understand what is right and what is wrong, and I can make her understand by signs what I mean."

Ellen Greaves' testimony and description of events was corroborated by Hannah Butcher, who said that from her observation as a married woman she believed the prisoner had been delivered of a child on the Friday.

Ann Briggs' evidence was crucial for Esther Dyson on three counts. Firstly, she was able to identify the green cloth in which the baby's body and head had been wrapped as being part of a sofa cover belonging to William Dyson, the prisoner's brother; secondly, she was able to tell the coroner's jury of the education that Esther had received from her over a period of twelve months about five or six years previously when she had taught Esther along with William and young Yeardley. In this instance, she was able to state that Esther Dyson was able to read and write better than many of her hearing, uneducated and illiterate neighbours and had enough intelligence to make herself understood by signs, and to understand other people who could sign to her. Finally, she described how she had questioned the prisoner several times in sign language, and how Esther had several times refuted her suggestion that the child's head

41

had been cut off and not pulled off during birth as she had insisted.

James Hinderson attested to his search of the Dyson house on the night of Sunday 26th September, and his discovery of the blood on the floor and walls of the bedroom that belonged to Esther Dyson, together with the blood-stained articles of clothing in her box. It was evident from his observations that the chamber window sill had been used as the board on which the child's head had been cut off. The blood found on the opposite wall could have been due to the head or the body being thrown across the room after severance and hitting the wall, causing blood to be sprayed and marking the wall.

Hinderson also stated that the prisoner had denied to him she had thrown the body into the water of the dam, but had merely laid it in.

He stated that he had known the prisoner and her brother well, and could communicate with them through sign language. They had worked in Ecclesfield Mill for eleven years - William continuously, and Esther periodically as work demanded, and he had responsibility for them as Overlooker in the mill. In his considered opinion, Esther Dyson was a shrewd and intelligent woman.

Hinderson's evidence was corroborated in part by James Machin, the vestry clerk, who attested that upon being requested to do so by James Hinderson, he had gone to the Dyson house and found it in the state described. He went on to state that as a consequence of information received, he had gone to the Cotton Mill Dam at daylight the next morning with William Shaw, the constable, and searched the dam, finding and pulling out the headless body of an infant female, wrapped in a green cloth identified as belonging to William Dyson.

A further search by other parties had turned up the severed head of the child.

William Shaw, the constable of Ecclesfield, confirmed the testimony of Machin and the finding of the body and its head.

There was a question raised as to how it came to be that the Cotton Mill Dam was identified as the place where the body of the child was to be found.

A witness, William Graham, testified that on the Saturday night at about 8 p.m. he had been returning home to Ecclesfield from Wortley when he met the prisoner in Lee Lane. They had passed within a yard of each other, and she had something wrapped up before her in her apron, and was walking at a fast pace and went on a footpath leading from Ecclesfield to Wortley about 600 yards from the cotton mill dam. The witness said the prisoner had tried to avoid him, but he had seen who it was.

Graham stated that about 40 yards further on he came up to Henry Woodhouse, another resident of Ecclesfield, who had said to him, "Was that not the Dumb girl I had seen?", and he had said that it was.

He gave this information to Mr.Machin and Constable Shaw the next evening after the story had gone round the township about the Dumb Girl and her bastard child.

Another witness, a servant named Fanny Guest, also attested that she had passed Esther Dyson, whom she recognised, on the same footpath near the cotton mill dam with something under her apron, and had also given that information to the village constable.

Having satisfied themselves as to how the body came to be discovered, the coroner's jury now heard evidence concerning the examination of the body and of the prisoner when held at the workhouse.

Sarah Ingham, the governess of Ecclesfield Workhouse, gave evidence of the delivery of the child's body to her premises and how Esther Dyson had been brought in to be confronted with the body. She stated the prisoner had repeated to her the same story she had told others, that the head had been torn off during delivery of the child because it had come out feet first, and she had tried to pull it out. Mrs.Ingham had challenged the prisoner on this, producing a knife and signing that she had cut the child's head off with a similar instrument. The prisoner had thrown herself on one side and shunned the idea.

The workhouse governess had the prisoner stripped, and her breasts examined, and found them to contain a great deal of milk.

Two surgeons, William Jackson and Joseph Campbell, gave evidence of their examination of the body.

Dr.Jackson stated that the head had been separated at the 5th and 6th cervical vertebrae, where the neck joined the chest. He attested that it could only have been cut off with a rough-edged knife, and that there was no possibility it could have been torn off or screwed off as stated by the mother.

He had also no doubt, from particular examinations of the child and its mother, that it had been born alive, and that the physical appearance of the mother showed clearly she had recently delivered a child.

Dr.Campbell, having also examined both the woman and the child, fully corroborated Dr.Jackson's testimony. He stated the child had been seven and a quarter pounds in weight.

The Coroner, Mr.B.Badger, summed up the findings and bade the jury to retire to consider their recommendations. After only a few minutes, they returned with a verdict against Esther Dyson of 'Wilful Murder'.

The Coroner then issued a warrant for the committal of Esther Dyson to York Castle, to await her trial at the next Assizes.

On 9th July 1831, the case came up before Mr. Justice J. Parke at York when Esther Dyson was indicted for the wilful murder of her bastard child by cutting off its head, and was also charged with the same offence upon the coroner's inquisition.

In the legal language of the day : 'she stood mute and a jury was impanneled to try whether she did so by malice, or by the visitation of God; and evidence having been given of her always being deaf and dumb, the jury found that she stood mute by the visitation of God.'

The learned judge then examined a male witness on oath who was acquainted with her, who swore that she could be made to understand some things by signs, and give her answers by signs. This witness was probably Thomas Yeardley, the owner of Ecclesfield Mill and the father of Esther's friend, the deaf Young Yeardley. He was the only male witness on the list of 13 witnesses called before the court who had not given any evidence at the Coroner's Inquiry, and who was also the only male witness apart from John Hinderson and William Dyson who had any knowledge of sign language at all, and it was not likely that these two would be chosen to interpret.

He was sworn as follows : "You swear that you will well and truly interpret and make known to the prisoner at the bar by such signs, ways and methods as shall be best known to you, the indictment and inquisition wherewith she stands charged; and also all such matters and things as the Court shall require to be made known to her; and also well and truly interpret to the Court the plea of the said prisoner to the said indictment and inquisition respectively, and all answers of the said prisoner to the said matters and things so required to be made known to her, according to the best of your skill and understanding - so help you God."

It was then explained to Esther Dyson by signs what she was charged with, to which she responded by signs which obviously imparted denials. This was done twice, once for the indictment and once for the inquisition, and Mr.Justice Parke then directed that a plea of Not Guilty be entered as the prisoner's plea to both counts.

The witness interpreting was then called upon to explain to the prisoner that she was to be tried by a jury, and that she would be allowed to respond in her defence as she wished. But he stated that he could not present sufficient argument to the witness or on her behalf as the accused was incapable of understanding or following the nature of the proceedings and making her defence according to law, although she was intelligent enough in the common occurrence of daily matters.

This testimony was concurred with by Ann Briggs who stated that she had instructed the prisoner previously using the deaf alphabet and by signs, but Esther Dyson was not so far advanced as to be capable of putting words together.

After other witnesses had given similar testimony as had been presented before the coroner's jury, Mr.Justice Parke instructed the jury that if the, the jury, were satisfied that the prisoner had not, due to being deaf and dumb, intelligence enough to understand the nature of the proceedings, they ought to find her not sane, but if they believed she had understanding of the proceedings and the nature of the crime she stood accused of, they ought to find her guilty.

The jury returned a verdict of guilty but not sane, and Esther Dyson was then ordered to be kept in strict custody in York Castle until his Majesty's pleasure be known.

(Author's note : There is a statement in a different hand on the back of the indictment in the Public Records Office, date unknown, indicating that Esther Dyson was released from prison on the personal recognisance of three individuals, one of whom was Thomas Yeardley. This statement is faded, and unclear.)

6 :   1875 Birmingham

A CHRISTMAS AFFRAY

Christmas in the Victorian era was a rough time for the poor who would often try to make their own amusement through drink or fights, and it was no different in the lodging house occupied by several young metalworkers at 13 Thomas Street in the Aston area of Birmingham on Christmas night, 1875 where several young men were having a drink when the door burst open and two youths entered the room.

One of them, whom the drinking youths knew by the name of Edward Walters, said aggressively, "There are three men in this town that want to do me, and I should like to fight one of them."

A young man living in the house named Joe Barnett asked, "Who is it?"

"It is Jimmy Brislin," Walters said, looking directly at another youth who was quietly drinking his beer.

"I am Jimmy Brislin," the drinking youth said as he stood up, and both youths then went out of the house into the street where a stand-up fight commenced, noisily encouraged by other youths surrounding them, some of whom had been drinking with Brislin.

After a few minutes, it was apparent that young Jimmy Brislin was not up to the challenge thrown down by Edward Walters. He was knocked down twice, and was getting the worse of the fight. One of Brislin's friends ran to a nearby pub where he knew that Brislin's father was drinking and reported the fight to him.

The father came out of the pub, and saw that his son was down on the road, and went over to pick him up at the same time the fight was broken up by two women who pushed away the aggressive Walters. One of them, Jane Robinson, helped the senior Brislin pick up his son, and advised him to take the boy home, pushing them up the street, over the protests of some of the other youths who saw their entertainment being taken away from them.

One of the furious youths, who had been the one with Walters when they went into the house to challenge Brislin, threw a punch at the father, hitting the older man in the mouth, before Mrs.Robinson managed to get them away into their house nearby.

"Tis a fine thing," said the elder Brislin angrily to Jane Robinson, "when I am hit on the mouth by a mere boy!"

Another youth, Frederick Humpage, who had been in the room with Jimmy Brislin earlier, returned to 13 Thomas Street and had only been in a minute when the boy who had punched the elder Brislin rushed into the room and took a bread knife out of a dish, and with the handle in his hand and the blade up his sleeve, the youth ran out again. Humpage followed him out into the yard, where the father, William Brislin was standing talking to a John Caldicott and the two women at the entry to an alleyway off Thomas Street.

Spotting that he was being followed, the youth turned upon Humpage and grabbed him by the collar of his jacket, and showing him the knife, made a motion of thrusting it. Letting go of Humpage, the youth then ran up the yard and was seen to wield a knife and strike William Brislin on the head twice. The stricken man staggered across the road and collapsed on the pavement, bleeding profusely.

The son, Jimmy Brislin, came out and pulled away the youth, making motions not to strike his father again, but the youth threw Brislin against a wall, and punched him in the side with the hand containing the knife, but did not stab him. The boy then ran away, followed by Humpage and Caldicott.

The police were called from the station over the road, and when police constable Ell and Detective Cooper arrived at the scene, they found Brislin lying in the street with terrible wounds on his head. On questioning witnesses, the policemen were given the description of the assailant who could be found living in a lodging house a few doors away from the Brislin house.

Upon calling and gaining entry to the house, the two police officers found Humpage and Caldicott standing at the foot of the stairs. Both indicated that the youth they wanted was upstairs, and upon searching the house, they found a youth hiding behind a bed in an upper room, from which hiding place he was dragged out and handcuffed and transported to the local police station. Other youths involved in the general disturbances were also arrested and transported to the police station.

Meanwhile, the wounded man, Brislin, was loaded into a cab called by Detective Cooper and transported to Birmingham General Hospital where his wounds were found to be serious.

At the police station, the youth who had been dragged out from behind a bed wrote down on a piece of paper, "Samuel Todd. Deaf and Dumb." The police were unable to question him further to their satisfaction, only gaining the impression from the prisoner's motions and signs that he had knocked down someone. However, their enquiries at the lodging house identified the youth as Samuel Todd, aged 18, employed as a filer in a local engineering company.

On Monday 27th December 1875, Todd appeared before magistrates at Birmingham Police Court along with another youth, Joseph Barnett, aged 21, a metal-roller at the same engineering works as Todd and who also resided in the same lodging house. Both were charged with causing an affray, and with grievous assault against William Brislin.

Magistrates found no case to answer against Joseph Barnett when the police could not produce any evidence that he had assaulted Brislin, and ordered his release. However, Samuel Todd was identified by several witnesses as one of the leading members of the group of youths who had assaulted Brislin, and in particular by John Caldicott as the one who had possessed a knife in the affray, and was remanded in custody until 5th January 1876.

However, William Brislin died of his injuries in hospital on 30th December, and Samuel Todd came up before the magistrates again on Saturday 1st January 1876. This time, the charge was murder!

Samuel Todd had been deaf from birth, and had been born in Ireland in 1857. For a period of six months, he had attended the Cabra Institution for the Deaf and Dumb in Dublin before running away from his family to Birmingham when he was 10 years old. For several years, he had earned his living as a filer.

In order to communicate with Todd, the police appealed for help from the Royal Institution for the Deaf and Dumb at Edgbaston, Birmingham who sent along a teacher named Wilson to assist the police. However, Wilson found that he was unable to understand fully the prisoner's Irish Sign Language and did not feel competent to stand as interpreter at the next magistrates sitting which took place on 14th January 1876. He explained to the Bench that it was with the greatest difficulty that he could either understand the prisoner or make the prisoner understand him. The accused had expressed himself sufficiently for him to be led to understand that he had been at an institution in Ireland for six months but had been without instruction since.

Detective Cooper, who had charge of the case, said a boy who formerly lived with the prisoner could apparently make himself understood by him. However, Wilson stated that the boy alluded to interpreted in so eccentric a fashion that he (Wilson) was not confident things were being so faithfully interpreted. In speaking of the fight, for instance, he did not believe the boy understood the prisoner to say what was in fact interpreted.

Detective Cooper said he had written on a piece of paper which the prisoner, upon seeing, motioned that he had only knocked the deceased down. Mr.Gem, magistrate's clerk, pointed out that different interpretations could be placed on such motions. The prisoner might either have meant he knocked Brislin down, or that he was knocked down by Brislin. As a test, the magistrate's clerk wrote on a piece of paper in bold handwriting and handed it to Todd. It read, "How old are you?"

Todd, after looking at it carefully for a few seconds, wrote underneath, "Samuel Todd" in very legible handwriting. It was remarked by the magistrates that it was strange that a lad who could write so well could not read a few simple words.

The Stipendiary, T.C.S.Kynnersley, then put a second test to the prisoner by writing down a sentence relating to the charge of murder. Upon reading it, Todd burst into tears, and the magistrate's clerk commented it was pretty evident that Todd could read after all, and Detective Cooper said he felt certain that Todd could read a newspaper.

The teacher Wilson disagreed, saying that Todd might be able to read a few simple words by spelling them out letter by letter but his knowledge could not be said to extend further than that.

It was then decided tat the court would make use of the boy stated to have lived with Todd, and he was sent for. It was said that this boy was reluctant to come to court as his mother was wanted for a felony. Nonetheless, he was found in nearby Thomas Street, and brought to the court and asked to identify himself.

"My name is John Parker," he said, "I have lived with the prisoner for eight years since he came over from Ireland."

Asked if he could converse with the prisoner, Parker said that they had developed over the years they lived together a means of communication through a sign language which he recognised differed from other native Birmingham Deaf people he had met.

Stipendiary Kynnersley decided that Parker would act as interpreter for Todd and would sit by his side in the dock, and that Mr.Wilson would watch them closely to check that there was nothing said that appeared to be attempts to deceive the court.

The court then proceeded to take evidence from witnesses.

Police Constable Ell and Detective Cooper recited the circumstances of the arrest, and how the prisoner had expressed himself through signs they he had knocked down William Brislin.

John Caldicott identified in the court Samuel Todd as the youth he had seen running up to the deceased in the alleyway entry brandishing a bread-knife and stabbing Brislin twice above the eye.

Frederick Humpage, Jimmy Brislin and Jane Robinson described the circumstances that led to the fight in the street, and the involvement of the deceased which led to his death. Humpage also described how he had seen

Samuel Todd take the bread knife, and how he had followed him out of the house, and how he himself had been threatened by Todd.

Stipendiary Kynnersley questioned a surgeon from Birmingham General Hospital, a Mr. Ottley, about the nature of the injuries suffered by Brislin. The surgeon stated that the post mortem showed that Brislin was not stabbed, as stated by the police, but had been struck above the right eye by a blunt weapon causing the skull to fracture. He agreed the weapon could be the handle of a knife, but in his view was more likely to be caused by a stone or even by striking his head on the road.

Through his interpreter Parker, Todd denied that he had possession of a knife or that he had attacked Brislin with a knife. He admitted to having thrown a stone and to knocking Brislin down *during the first fracas* immediately after the fight in Thomas Street, and to being part of a group of youths who were running up Thomas Street later that night when Brislin had met his death but denied knocking him down during that second fracas.

The magistrates found that there was a case to prove against Samuel Todd, and he was committed accordingly to trial, which took place at the next summer Assizes in Warwick.

The same witnesses were called at the trial, and John Parker was again asked to be the prisoner's interpreter, much to the disgust of the teacher William Wilson, who in his statement to the Judge firmly disassociated himself from any accuracy in the interpretation or statements made by the prisoner.

As was usual for trials involving Deaf people at this time, the issues revolved round the fitness of Samuel Todd to plead to the indictment, and his ability to understand the charges against him.

Samuel Todd was found guilty but insane and was sentenced to imprisonment "..until Her Majesty's pleasure be known..."

In closing the case, the Judge thanked all the witnesses for their contribution to the case, and directed that each of them including...."..the boy Parker be paid £40 each .."

This may be the first record of any fee paid to a sign language interpreter.

7 : 1888 Cardiff, Wales

A KILLING BY TETANUS!

Friday the 17th of July 1888 was a hot summer's day in Cardiff, South Wales and the Ely river, which flows through the western suburbs of the Welsh capital, proved to be an attraction that was irresistible to many young children as a means of cooling off in the heat.

In the fields on both sides of the river below the Ely Bridge, groups of boys gathered to frolic in the river, and boys being boys, some horseplay began which developed into a fairly nasty throwing contest between different groups on opposite sides of the river. It seemed to onlookers that the main target of a large group of boys on one side of the river was an unfortunate individual on the opposite bank who was being belted with clumps of mud, turf and dirt.

After one particularly large clump of dirt which was thrown by one of the more aggressive individuals scored a direct hit on the face of the other unfortunate individual, the latter lost his temper and picked up a stone and aimed it at his tormentor.

The stone missed its intended target, but a loud scream from another boy standing nearby who had taken no part in the taunting indicated to onlookers that the stone had found a target and hurt someone.

Henry William Davies, aged 11, the son of a bricklayer George Davies, had received a nasty blow on his right knee causing it to bleed, and he limped off crying profusely to his home in Canton, Cardiff arriving at half-past six and told his mother, Emma Davies, that "a deaf and dumb boy" had thrown a stone at him at the river at Ely Bridge.

56

His mother bathed the wound, which was an open cut about an inch and a quarter long, in warm water and applied to it a bread poultice. Her son stayed in the house the rest of the evening, but the next day, feeling better, young Henry Davies went out to play.

It was one week later, on Friday 25th July, that Emma Davies was startled by a cry from her son's bedroom, followed by a thud, and ran upstairs to find him on the bed in convulsions. Alarmed, she sent for the local doctor, Joseph James.

The doctor examined young Henry's open wound, and suspected from the convulsions that tetanus had set in.

Henry Davies died the next day in agony, At times, his body was arched off the bed with only his head and heels touching it as the tetanus overcame him.

Dr.James reported the death to the local coroner, Mr.James Reece, who immediately ordered that a post mortem examination be carried out to determine the cause of death. Dr.James found during the post mortem that apart from the one and quarter-inch wound, there was no other mark on the boy and all the internal organs were healthy apart from the congestion due to the spasms caused by the tetanus. He determined the cause of death to be tetanus produced by the wound to the knee.

On the following Monday evening, at the Market Hotel, Canton, Cardiff, the district coroner James Reece held an inquest into the death of the young boy. The inquest heard evidence from a boy named William Robert Loud, aged 17, of 17 Loftus St, Canton that he had been in a field on the same side of the river as the deceased and had seen a boy named Llewellyn, with others, throwing stones and dirt at another boy whose name was Draper on the other side of the river. The boy Draper was hit in the face with a piece of dirt, but Loud had not seen who had thrown that particular piece of dirt. As a result of that, Draper had picked up a stone and aimed it at Llewellyn who had thrown most stones at Draper. He had heard a loud "Oh!" behind him, and turned round to see the deceased crying and his leg bleeding.

After hearing from Dr.Joseph James that death had occurred as a consequence of the wound suffered by the boy Davies, the wound producing tetanus, the Coroner instructed the jury that if they believed the evidence, they had no alternative but to charge the boy Draper with manslaughter. The jury duly returned a verdict of manslaughter against the boy Draper.

At this, a woman collapsed in an hysterical fit. This woman was Elizabeth Draper, the accused boy's mother.

What happened next was a bit of a farce. On Wednesday 30th July, William Henry Draper, aged 15, an uneducated Deaf youth without any speech was arraigned before Cardiff police court with Mr.T.W.Lewis, Stipendiary, presiding, assisted by Dr.Paine, charged with causing the death of Henry William Davies, aged 11, by striking him on the leg with a stone thus producing a tetanus infection.

Draper was undefended, and no-one had thought to arrange for an interpreter to ensure that he could follow the proceedings.

To make matters further complicated, a police inspector named Lewis had just commenced giving evidence when he was stopped by the magistrates' clerk and informed that the prosecution was being tried in the wrong court. The place where the stone throwing had taken place was by a few yards within the jurisdiction of the county police who should properly be handling the prosecution. Inspector Lewis protested that the death had in fact taken place within the boundaries of the city of Cardiff, but the Stipendiary informed him that that was irrelevant, and remanded the prisoner in the custody of the county police for them to begin the prosecution if so warranted. The Stipendiary also made the point that it was essential the defendant be allowed a sign language interpreter.

In the week that followed, the county police at Llandaff took over the prosecution, and engaged Alexander Melville, Principal of the School for the Deaf and Dumb, also situated in Llandaff, as interpreter for the boy.

Although the Llandaff School had been in existence since 1862, Melville found that William Draper had never been to his or any other school or institution in existence where deaf children could be educated. He also found that Draper was unknown to other Deaf people in the locality, never having mixed with them, and consequently could not make himself understood to the boy at first, nor could he understand the boy's own sign language so by trial and error, the two gradually developed some means of communication, helped by the boy's mother.

William Draper appeared in court for the second time on Monday 4th June 1888, this time at the Llandaff police court before Messrs. C.H.Williams and E.Lewis. He was again undefended, but had this time Melville as interpreter.

The court heard, as had the coroner's inquiry, evidence from Dr.Joseph James of the results of the post mortem which showed that tetanus had been the cause of death. Dr.James stated that he had been called in by Mrs.Davies on the Friday 25th July and had diagnosed lockjaw, and had feared for the boy Davies through the convulsions and spasms that followed but had done all he could to ease the pain.

Two boys, a William Loud - who had given evidence at the coroner's inquiry - and a Albert Jones, alias Llewellyn, aged 12, gave evidence of a group of boys throwing things at Draper on the opposite bank. Llewellyn stated he did not see Draper throw anything back, but Loud asserted Draper had thrown a stone at the deceased.

Another boy, Edward Ernest Morgan of 21 Pen-y-poed Street, Canton, aged 10, said that he had accompanied Draper, whom he sometimes went round with, to the Ely river on the day in question and had been on the same side of the river as Draper when some boys on the opposite bank started throwing turf, dirt and stones at the pair of them. A boy called Jones or Llewellyn had been doing most of the throwing but Draper had not retaliated until he was hit in the face with a particularly large clump of dirt, and in his anger, had picked up a small-ish stone and aimed his throw at Jones but missed. The stone hit another boy standing nearby who had taken no part in the stone-throwing, and he had seen that boy cry and limp off. He and Draper had then left the riverbank to get away from the other boys.

Emma Davies, the dead boy's mother, related how her son had come home that evening crying bitterly and blaming his wound on a "deaf and dumb boy" who had thrown a stone at him. She stated that although the wound had been open all the time, it had she thought not been causing any harm and her son had not complained until one week afterwards, on the 25th, when he collapsed in pain, and she had sent for Dr.James who attended to him until her son died the next day in convulsions.

Inspector Lewis of the city police related how the case had been brought to his attention, and how his enquiries had led to the suspect being identified as Draper, who had been arrested following the charge made at the coroner's inquiry.

There was quite an absurd allegation that Draper had a knife on him at the time and had used it (although how he could get from one side of the river to the other to do the stabbing and still not be seen by a multitude of other boys was not stated). Draper denied having had a knife and this was confirmed by his friend Edward Morgan and the matter was not pursued.

Elizabeth Draper, the mother of the accused, told the court that her son had been deaf and dumb since the age of two when he had fallen down the stairs, and had never been to any school. She stated that she could not make him understand anything about the case.

Her view was supported by Alexander Melville, acting as interpreter, who stated that he doubted if the prisoner had any intelligent idea what was going on in the court, and it would be impossible to make him understand that he was at liberty to make a statement in his own behalf.

The magistrates, however, found that there was a case for Draper to answer, and committed him to the next Assizes at Swansea. Alexander Melville was requested to act as interpreter.

He was to write later in Llandaff School Annual Report for 1889 that "owing to the boy's entire want of education, and his never mixing with the deaf and dumb, his 'signs' were extremely meagre and crude, so that it was impossible to make him understand the nature of the proceedings. The Bench had decided to send the case to the Assizes at Swansea and I was bound over to appear as interpreter.

"On the case being called and the jury sworn. I represented to his lordship that the prisoner was incapable of understanding the nature of the proceedings and could not plead, whereupon the judge proceeded to impannel the jury to say whether the prisoner stood mute by the act of God or of malice. On being sworn, I repeated the evidence I had already given, viz. , that the unfortunate youth was incapable of pleading to the indictment, and that he stood mute by the act of God, whereupon the jury brought in a verdict accordingly."

William Draper was then sentenced to be kept in confinement during Her Majesty's pleasure. However, representations were made to the Home Secretary regarding the harshness of the sentence and the unusual and unique method of manslaughter through causing a tetanus infection, and the boy was released after a short confinement into his mother's charge.

Alexander Melville went on to slam the waste of money involved in the prosecution, saying in his report :"Altogether the case cost the county more money than would have educated the lad, while his poor father died of vexation." [In those days, placement of children, especially deaf children, in special schools rested upon local school boards who had to decide whether they were justified in using some of their budget to send away children out of their boundaries to be educated. Despite the fact that the Llandaff School for the Deaf and Dumb was only in the next parish to that where Draper lived, it appears that funding was refused for him to be sent there.]

8 : 1893 Leicester

A VINDICTIVE WIFE

The noise of the gunshot in the early hours of the bitterly cold morning of 17th February 1893 in Upper Hill, Leicester, startled neighbours and the few pedestrians who had braved the cold weather.

The sudden silence that followed momentarily was soon shattered by the screaming of a woman who ran out of the house at 22 Upper Hill into the dark street, bleeding heavily on the left side of the head.

A police officer, P.C. Dobney, who had heard the sound of the gunshot hurried quickly to the scene outside the entrance of the house, which was beginning to attract curious but fearful neighbours and passers-by.

The terrified and hysterical woman reappeared after a few minutes and went straight into the reassuring arms of the policeman at the scene. A few moments later, a man came out of the building, holding a revolver in his hand. P.C. Dobney immediately grabbed hold of the man, taking away the gun from his hand, and placed him under arrest.

The woman was admitted to Leicester Infirmary, where the house surgeon, Mr.W.G.Roll, attended to a small wound on the left side of the head, about two and three quarters of an inch above the ear. The wound was not life-threatening, and the house surgeon noticed that the woman also had bruising around her eyes.

The next day, Alfred E.Harris, aged 26, described as a hawker living at 22 Upper Hill, Leicester, appeared before Leicester Magistrates at the Town Hall, charged with the attempted murder of his wife, Minnie Harris. The Chief Constable opposed the application for bail, and the prisoner was committed to the Borough of Leicester Prison to await trial at the next Assizes.

The *Leicester Mercury*, in reporting the committal, stated that Harris was a Deaf-mute.

Alfred Harris was a well-known and popular man in the Deaf community of Leicester, pitied by some for having married in June 1892 a hearing woman who treated him shabbily and spent frivolously all the money that he earned. Minnie Harris, a domestic servant at a wealthy family's house on Narborough Road, Leicester, was regarded as a quarrelsome and bad-tempered woman who had already left her husband on four previous occasions following rows, mostly about money, and had only returned to him on the night of the shooting.

The Deaf community of Leicester believed that Alfred Harris was innocent of the charge of attempted murder, that he had in fact been trying to take away the revolver from his wife during another of their rows about money when the gun had accidentally gone off and wounded her in the head. They believed that Minnie Harris had vindictively turned the situation to her advantage to get rid of her husband. Through the pages of the *Leicester Mercury*, eight Leicester Deaf adults launched an appeal for a fighting fund to ensure proper representation for Harris during his trial.

The appeal was repeated in the April issue of the magazine *British Deaf-Mute*, asking Missioners for the Deaf throughout Britain to respond and collect contributions from their church congregations.

The appeal was supported by a letter written by another Leicester Deaf adult : 'I went to prison yesterday, but Harris declined to see anybody, he is low-spirited and, as the rules of the prison do now allow a person on trial to be employed in any work and no books to read, only an half-hour daily allowed for exercise, you cannot wonder that the solitary forced seclusion is telling on him. In fact I fear he will lose his reason before the trial. Time hangs wearily enough on an hearing person, but, oh, who but fellow creatures similarly afflicted can understand or feel the horrible condition of a deaf in Harris' position. Could not some representation be made to the Home Secretary? Ought we not to take some steps, making Harris' case a test one to secure employment, or at least some consideration to break the monotonous existence a deaf-mute must lead, who is committed for trial. I declare at present Harris is undergoing a terrible punishment before he has been tried, and am also certain that his present position will have a detrimental effect on him lifelong. I have spoken to the prison warders, but they can do nothing in the matter. His diet is 12 oz. of bread and one pint of coffee daily. We have to send him food or he would starve.'

Another letter-writer thundered : 'I have made minute and searching enquiries about Harris, investigated and examined evidence on both sides, and although he is encompassed with a chain or circumstantial evidence which undoubtedly appears to be very black against him, I AM THOROUGHLY CONVINCED HARRIS IS INNOCENT. The evidence which we present possess in the hands of a good counsel, will without doubt prove him innocent of the crime of which he is accused. Here is the case in a few words - an half-educated Deaf-Mute, without friends and without money, accused of the worse of crimes, with the blackest of evidence piled up against him; and who is in my opinion and in the opinion of the Deaf of Leicester innocent.'

Although the appeal brought forth contributions from many of the leading Deaf people in the country, it was not as well supported as hoped by those who had launched the appeal.

The trial of Alfred Ernest Harris took place on 3rd July 1893 at Leicester Assizes on an indictment of shooting at Minnie Harris, his wife, with a loaded revolver, with intend, feloniously, wilfully and of his malice aforethought, to kill and murder her on 17th February. Sign language interpretation was provided by the wife of the local Leicester Missioner, J.W.Pound.

Minnie Harris was the first to give evidence, and under questioning by the prosecutor, Mr.Toller, she stated that she had first left her husband three weeks after their marriage the preceding June because he had threatened her.

The Judge : "How did he express his threats if he was deaf and dumb?"

Mrs. Harris : "With a knife."

The Judge : "He shook a knife at you?"

Mrs. Harris : "Yes, because I did not give him my money."

Continuing her evidence, Mrs.Harris stated that they had been apart for five months, then had lived together again. She had left him once more after he had tried to strangle her and had lived apart for some time. They had got back together for about two or three weeks when she left him again after he had struck her. To keep herself, she had entered service as a domestic servant at a house in Narborough Road where she had received several letters from Alfred Harris in February 1893 asking her to go back to him. This she did on the evening of 17th February, and had gone to bed at about ten o'clock.

Describing what happened afterwards, Minnie Harris testified that she was just dozing off to sleep when she saw a flash and the prisoner hit her on the right eye. She put up her hands to defend herself, then felt a revolver in

Alfred Harris' hand. In a struggle, she managed to get hold of it and throw it away. He got his knees into her back and tried to suffocate her by holding one hand over her mouth and pinching her nose. He tried to strangle her with both hands on her neck. She had managed to scream 'Murder!', get off the bed and run to the door where her husband caught up with her and pushed her from the top to the bottom of the staircase. She had managed to get out into the street where she found she had a wound on the left side of her head, and was bleeding from it and from her mouth and nose as well. She went into a closet for some time, and then returned to the street where she found a policeman who had her taken to the Infirmary.

Cross-examined by defence counsel Mr.Lindsell, she testified that she had left her husband four times in total, and insisted it was always he who had tried to make her go back to him.

Mr. W.G.Roll, the house surgeon who had treated Mrs. Harris at the Infirmary, testified that she had been admitted suffering from a small wound on the left side of her head. It was such a wound as could have been caused by the bullets produced in court. The wound was not life-threatening. He had also noticed bruising around her eyes.

In cross examination, Mr. Roll stated that the wound was about three-quarters of an inch in depth, and the bone had not been fractured. He was of the opinion that the bullet had bounced off Mrs.Harris's head. If it had continued its course, it would have gone through the skull.

Benjamin Vaughan, a hawker living next door to Alfred Harris, said that on the night in question, he had heard the report of a firearm followed about a minute afterwards by screams of 'Murder'. There were then sounds of a struggle in the room, and the noise of someone going down the stairs very hastily, not walking down them. He had got dressed and come out into the street in time to see P.C. Dobney place Harris under arrest.

P.C. Dobney testified that he had heard the gunshot, and had arrested the prisoner when he exited from his house carrying a gun in his right hand. He had grabbed hold of the prisoner's right arm, and forced him to drop the revolver. It was a six-chambered weapon, five chambers of which were still loaded and there was evidence that the sixth chamber had been discharged and the weapon recently used.

P.C. Dobney stated that when Mrs.Harris came back to the house, she had said, : 'You have done this. Give me back the money you have taken from my purse.'

Cross-examined by Mr.Lindsell for the defence, P.C. Dobney testified that he had let off one chamber of the revolver by accident. It had gone off easily with little pressure.

A witness named as Alfred Rutt from Northampton briefly testified that the revolver and a quantity of cartridges had been purchased from him by Alfred Harris in the first week of February.

Mrs. Harris was then recalled to the witness stand by the defence and subjected to a most severe cross-examination by Mr. Lindsell as to her reasons for accusing her husband of taking her money. When pressed for a reply to a question, she fainted, and was carried from the court.

Presenting the case for the defence, Mr.Lindsell pointed out the disadvantage under which the prisoner laboured, and contended that he was at the mercy of a vindictive woman. It was clear that she had not been a good wife to him, that they did not live on good terms. She had,

Mr.Lindsell said, left him four times and was plainly a quarrelsome and bad-tempered woman who was the real case of the unhappiness between the two of them and he asked the jury to look at the case in this light, and not to believe the evidence presented that the man had bought the revolver for the purpose of shooting his wife. If Alfred Harris had really wanted to kill his wife, he could have quite easily done so but the evidence showed that the shot was not fired directly at her. It was not possible to believe the doctor's opinion that the bullet had just bounced off Mrs. Harris's skull.

Mr.Lindsell maintained that the wife had enormously and maliciously exaggerated what had happened on the night of the shooting. If there had been any truth in her story, there would have been more marks on her. He suggested that there had been a quarrel on the night in question, as there had often been before, and during the quarrel and struggle which followed, Mrs. Harris had taken up the revolver, and in trying to get it off her, the gun had gone off by accident. The jury had heard from the witness P.C. Dobney how easily this could be done. The wound had been caused by an accident pure and simple, not with malice aforethought to murder.

Evidence of the prisoner's character was presented by his father, and by P.C. Walker, and the Judge then read out part of a statement which Alfred Harris wrote out.

"I can say nothing but the truth. I only bought the revolver for self-defence. It is very true that she took it out of my pocket, but say nothing at all in the bedroom. I did my very best to take it from her, but not until it went off. I am very sorry it hurt her. I give her 7 shillings to over £1 a day, but she spent it in two hours, or took it somewhere to be kept."

The Judge remarked that the statement went on to other matters which he did not think he ought to read. The main point of the statement was the suggestion that the revolver had gone off by accident.

The jury found Alfred Ernest Harris guilty of intent to murder, but made a recommendation to mercy on account of his deafness.

The Judge (to Mrs. Pound, the interpreter) : "Tell the prisoner the jury have found him guilty of shooting with intent to murder his wife. This is a very serious offence, but in passing sentence upon him, I shall take into consideration his affliction and I hope and I intend that those in charge of him in prison shall take that into consideration also. But I must pass upon him a severe sentence, and that sentence is that he be kept in penal servitude for five years."

9 : 1953 Carmarthen, Wales

AN UNWELCOME GUEST

The ancient township of Laugharne stands on the west shore of the River Taff where it starts to broaden out into Carmarthen Bay, about 15 miles by road from the county seat of Carmarthen in West Wales. It is in reality little more than a village of old cottages where many people were related to and knew each other, and would feel safe leaving their doors open all hours. There was hardly any crime in Laugharne - indeed, there had never been a murder in living memory in the locality.

This insularity was to be shattered on Saturday evening 10th January 1953 a passer-by in Clifton Street heard screams coming from the 100-year old cottage where an elderly spinster named Elizabeth Thomas resided. The passer-by reported the incident to the local constabulary, and Police Sergeant T.J.Morgan responded to the routine call. Upon arriving at the cottage, he could not get any answer to his knocking, and decided to force open the front door and made the shocking discovery of the elderly victim lying in the passageway in a pool of blood.

An ambulance was called, and transported the woman to Carmarthen Hospital where she died the following morning without recovering consciousness.

Meanwhile, back at the century-old cottage in Laugharne, Sergeant Morgan had reported his discovery to his superiors, and within a short time, two senior police officers, Superintendent John from the Carmarthen police headquarters, and Detective Inspector William Lloyd, head of Carmarthenshire C.I.D. were on the scene, followed almost immediately by the Chief Constable of Carmarthenshire, Mr.T. Hubert Lewis, who had been

71

called away from a private function he was attending, and was still in evening dress.

He announced to reporters that foul play was suspected, and as was the custom in those days, the Chief Constable after consultation with his senior police officers, decided to call in Scotland Yard, and that night, two detectives of the famed Scotland Yard Murder Squad found themselves travelling to Carmarthen.

The senior detective of the pair, Chief Superintendent Reginald Spooner was one of Scotland Yard's most famous detectives and had only recently just returned to London from the successful five-month investigation into the murder of Mrs. Alice Mary Maud Wiltshire, wife of a rich pottery manufacturer, at her home in Barleston, Staffordshire.

He was accompanied by his able assistant, Detective Sergeant E.Millen. Upon arrival in Carmarthen, they were taken straight to the murder scene in a police car provided by the Carmarthenshire Constabulary for their use.

By that time, it had been established by the local constabulary that the victim, Elizabeth Thomas, had last been seen in the little front room cottage shop across the road from her home, owned by grocer and confectioner J.F.Phillips, at 5.30 p.m. where she had purchased a quarter-pound of peppermints, her favourite sweets, and had gone through to the kitchen where she chatted to Mr.Phillips for a few minutes, and observed his wife preparing a boiled egg for their daughter's tea. She had said to the grocer and confectioner, "I think I'll go home now and have a boiled egg for tea myself," and with that parting remark, had left the shop to cross the road to her cottage.

That had been the last occasion anyone, except for her killer, had seen her alive, and it was a few minutes later that the passer-by had heard screams coming from her cottage and reported it to the local station.

The body had been found by Sergeant Morgan at 6.10 p.m., so a bare 40 minutes had elapsed since she had spoken to the grocer in his small shop across the road.

Chief Superintendent Spooner was not at all happy to learn that the local police had failed to secure the crime scene effectively, and had allowed some villagers into the cottage both to help with the removal of the victim to the ambulance, and to search the place for evidence of any other disturbance, before cordoning off the scene. Indeed, one of Miss Thomas's nephews, a Gordon Perkins, had been allowed to check the cottage and search for the victim's savings, which was known to be secreted somewhere in the house. These savings, over £200 in envelopes and paper bags, were found intact under the mattress in the main bedroom.

Forensic experts from the South Wales Police laboratories at Cardiff, led by a Chief Inspector Goodsall, a fingerprint expert, were called in only after the crime scene had been extensively contaminated by villagers crowding into the cottage.

Nonetheless, they spent a considerable time at the scene, and carried away many articles from the crime scene back to the forensic laboratories at Llanishen, Cardiff, for further examination.

House-to-house enquiries continued throughout the Sunday and Monday as police sought to piece together the victim's last movements and search for the murder weapon, which was not in the cottage. Police did not specify what the murder weapon was.

It was learnt that earlier that Saturday, Miss Thomas had watched a wedding take place in Laugharne Parish Church. It was also learnt that it was Miss Thomas's habit to leave the front and back doors half open most of the time like many other neighbours, so there would have been easy access by the murderer into the cottage, perhaps even when Miss Thomas had been in the grocer's shop. Perhaps she had surprised the intruder when she returned to her cottage.

Aged 77 at the time of her death, Elizabeth Thomas had lived alone since the death of her brother two years previously. Indeed, many of the cottages on her row were occupied by single, elderly people, and most of them also had the habit of leaving their doors open, so safe had they considered themselves in Laugharne.

For over 50 years, the victim had worked as a house-servant for a Mrs. Brayshay at the Glen, Laugharne, who described the victim as a quiet, unassuming person and a hard worker with a cheerful manner. She was also the cleaner and caretaker of St.Martin's Parish Church, Laugharne which she attended regularly, and had taken an active part in the local Women's Institute activities.

At a press conference on Monday morning, the Chief Constable, Mr. Lewis, flanked by Chief Superintendent Spooner and Superintendent John, appealed to anyone who could assist the police in their enquiries to come forward. "It may be that people who were in the vicinity of Clifton Street about 6 p.m. last Saturday, the approximate time the crime was committed, could give some information that could be of value." The Chief Constable confirmed that several men had been questioned by the police but that there had been no significant developments as yet.

At an inquest conducted by the coroner for West Carmarthen, Mr. W.D.Williams, on Monday evening, 12th January, formal identification of the body only was presented and the inquest provisionally adjourned to 28th January.

On Sunday evening, 18th January, Chief Superintendent Spooner called a press conference to announce that a man had been formally charged with the murder of Miss Elizabeth Thomas, and that this person would appear before the magistrates' court at St.Clear, Carmarthenshire the next morning.

In a hearing that lasted just six minutes, Mrs. Ceri Davies, wife of Beddoe Davies, the principal officer of the Deaf and Dumb Institute at Llanelli, stood beside the magistrates' clerk, and interpreted the proceedings in sign language for a man in the dock standing accused of the murder of Elizabeth Thomas.

The man, identified in court as George Roberts, aged 46, of Ferry House, Laugharne, nodded his head indicating that he understood what was being said.

Evidence of arrest was given by Police Superintendent D.J.John of Carmarthen who stated that at 5.30 p.m., in the presence of Chief Superintendent Spooner of the Scotland Yard Murder Squad, he formally charged Roberts with the murder of Elizabeth Thomas. "I formally charged him," said the superintendent, "and he replied 'I understand. That is all I have to say.' He was then taken into custody in Carmarthen and detained."

The superintendent asked for a remand until 27th January, and this was granted. The magistrates also granted a certificate of legal aid to Roberts.

So began a case that was to have far-reaching repercussions not only on the British legal system, but also in the United States where it was pivotal in the long, legal battle to free a Black male detained for the murder of a prostitute without a proper trial.

The trial of George Roberts, a born-Deaf handyman, opened at Cardiff Assizes on March 23rd 1953 before Mr. Justice Devlin (later to become the Chief Lord Justice). The Crown was represented by Vincent Lloyd-Jones, Q.C., assisted by Mr.J.Jones-Roberts, whilst the defence team was led by Edmund Davies, Q.C. assisted by Havard Evans and Hywel ap Roberts. Unlike the earlier appearances at the magistrates' courts, the defendant did not, on instruction by the defence team, have a sign language interpreter to follow the trial.

For the prosecution, Vincent Lloyd-Jones opened two hours legal argument as to whether the defendant Roberts was fit to stand trial for the murder, and evidence was called by the defence, which was not challenged by the prosecution, to show that Roberts had been deaf and without speech since birth. The jury, as was usual practice, was then impanelled to decide whether he was mute by malice or by visitation of God.

The jury found that George Roberts was mute by visitation of God, and the prosecution then submitted that the evidence so far called raised a presumption of idiotism; that, prima facie, the accused was unfit to plead, and incapable of following the proceedings, or of instructing counsel for the defence, or challenging a juror, and that these were the next issues that had to be tried.

The prosecution, said Lloyd-Jones, would call evidence of three doctors who had examined Roberts and would attest to his unfitness to plead. It was common ground that, if an accused was found unfit to plead, the learned judge must order his detention as a Broadmoor patient until Her Majesty's pleasure be known (which in theory meant life imprisonment without trial).

"What you are asking," Mr.Justice Devlin told the prosecution, "would mean that if I find the accused unfit to plead, I have to make an order under the Statute as a result of which he would be detained as a criminal lunatic and it would preclude any inquiry by the jury as to his guilt or not. In other words, it does not matter if he is guilty or not guilty, he is found to be a criminal lunatic anyway."

Mr. Lloyd-Jones : "The trial ought not to proceed until any presumption of idiotism has been displaced."

Mr.Justice Devlin : "Suppose the defence is, 'We agree our client is an idiot or a lunatic, and we cannot take any instructions from him, but we are able to put forward a witness who, if it is believed, can prove that our client was 10 miles away at the time of the crime, and therefore cannot have committed it?'"

Mr.Lloyd-Jones: "It is a paradoxical situation, I agree, but it seems to be supported by a certain amount of historical precedent," and went on to quote previous case histories, including the cases of Dyson, Pritchard and others.

The defence team submitted that the prosecution had no case to prove, and that the general issue should be tried first, to prove the accused guilty or not guilty, and his fitness to plead be taken into consideration by the jury, quoting the case of *Regina v. Berry*, 1876, as their point.

Mr.Justice Devlin adjourned for lunch, during which he would make a ruling on the case.

Following the lunch adjournment, the judge delivered a ruling which was to be a landmark decision for future cases : In this case the defendant has been found to be mute by the visitation of God on the verdict of a jury, and principle and authority direct that, unless there be some reason for taking some other course, that finding should be the basis of entering a plea of Not Guilty on behalf of the defendant and the trial against him must proceed. But whether the defendant is found mute by malice or by visitation of God, a question often arises at the beginning

77

of a trial whether he is fit to plead, and it has clearly been laid down by the authorities that, if it be established that a man's mind is such that he would be incapable of understanding the nature of the proceedings, it would not be right that he should be put on his trial and convicted of the offence. Such a conviction would not stand. It is clear from the authorities that it is not merely defects of the mind that may bring about that result. Defects of the senses, whether or not combined with some defect of the mind, may do so and the authorities are clear that, if there are no certain means of communication with the defendant so that there are no certain means of making sure he will follow as much as it is necessary that he should follow the proceedings at his trial, then he should be found unfit to plead.

"In this case...the question which has arisen is whether that is a matter which has to be determined by a jury at (the start of the trial)... or whether it can be tried and determined by the jury together with the trial and determination of the general issue (i.e. unfitness to plead determined during the trial) whether the defendant be Guilty or Not Guilty.

"Counsel for the defence wishes the general issue to be tried. He has not disclosed, as of course he is not bound to disclose, and indeed should not have disclosed, what the nature of his defence is. It may well be that the defence is that the prosecution witnesses do not make out a prima facie case, or it may be that the defence has other witnesses, not yet called, who if they be believed would destroy the case which the prosecution would otherwise have made out...Counsel for the defence, although he cannot be instructed by the defendant, may say : 'I do not think the prosecution can make any case against the defendant. If it can, then of course, I am in no position to defend it with his aid because he cannot instruct me and cannot tell his story. But if the prosecution can make out no case, then I am not prepared to let the matter go merely on the issue whether he is fit or unfit to plead'. If that issue is tried, and tried alone, and a verdict is returned by the jury that the defendant is unfit to plead, the court has no power except to make one order, viz. that he should be detained as a criminal lunatic, or Broadmoor patient as it is now called, until Her Majesty's pleasure be made known, which means of course for an indefinite period.

"Counsel for the defence cannot be forced to accept that course for his client if, on a true view of the facts, he thinks he can obtain for his client properly a verdict of Not Guilty. Nor can he be forced to elect. He must be entitled to retain his right to say that the defendant is not in a position to give him instructions and therefore, he cannot put him in the witness box to tell his own story. He cannot be forced to say to himself : 'Shall I play for safety and obtain a verdict whereby the defendant is detained as a criminal lunatic, or shall I gamble on the chance of my being able to get him off altogether, with the knowledge that if my gamble fails, he will be convicted of murder and there is only one sentence the court can pass, i.e. the death penalty.... To insist on the issue of being tried on the fitness to plead or not might result in the grave injustice of detaining as a criminal lunatic a man who was innocent, and, indeed, might result in the public mischief that a person so detained would be assumed in the eyes of the police and the authorities to have been the person responsible for the crime - whether he was or was not - and investigations which might have led to the apprehension of the true criminal would not take place.

"It cannot, I think, be our law that, by some formality of procedure, counsel for the defence should be prevented from (being able to submit evidence his client did not commit the crime) before the jury and so achieving for his client, if he can, a verdict of Not Guilty."

Mr.Justice Devlin then directed that the clerk of the court read out the indictment charging Roberts with murder, and directed that a plea of not guilty be entered, and the trial proceed on the general issue. The jury were then sworn, and Roberts' counsel, Edmund Davies was invited to challenge the jurors but chose not to do so.

The evidence for the prosecution included several statements alleged to have been made by the defendant, and the defence counsel objected to this evidence on the ground that the defendant could not have made, and did not make, these statements which were in any case obtained under circumstances where the defendant was under no official caution.

These statements, coupled with the fact that Roberts had been seen shortly before and after the murder, and the fact that he was known to have been in previous possession of a knife, were the only evidence the prosecution had to offer against Roberts. The defence made it clear they felt the evidence was very flimsy and weak - Roberts after all lived in the locality so had every right to be about the village, and he was a handyman by trade and naturally carried some of the tools of his trade, and the victim had not been killed by any knife according to the post mortem.

At the start of the second morning of the trial, Vincent Lloyd-Jones told the court that after consultation with the defence, the prosecution had decided not to offer any further evidence in the trial.

Mr.Justice Devlin commented, "That is a very proper course," then addressing the jury, said, "This man was taken to Carmarthen Police Station on the night of 10-11 January after the crime, and he was kept there until January 14. No charge of any sort had been made against him, and during that time he was questioned and questioned in a manner that was not designed merely to elicit facts, but was in the nature of a cross-examination. Being then released, he made a further purported statement on the 18th and it was only after that he was charged with the offence.

"I am conscious of the fact that the police have a very difficult task to discharge. It is very easy to criticise the way they discharge their duties. This case must have no doubt created at every stage difficult problems for them, but I would like to make this abundantly clear. There is no power in this country for any police officer to take persons into custody for questioning. A man cannot be detained unless he is arrested. It is of first importance that when any abuse of this practice, whether innocent or not, is brought to the notice of the court, it should be very carefully scrutinised. It is obvious that detaining a man three nights in a police station is open to misconstruction." The judge referred to the total absence of clues normally found in such cases of Roberts, and stressed to the jury that Roberts was not being freed because of a technical reason. No jury could return a verdict of guilty on the evidence the prosecution had to offer against Roberts. "I think," he said, "counsel for the prosecution was only anticipating the inevitable. There appears to be nothing in the circumstances of the case that point to the accused."

Turning to the prosecuting counsel, Mr. Lloyd-Jones, the judge said, "There is one little matter that disturbs me.

81

You did not open with details of the circumstances in which Roberts was taken to the police station and made statements."

Mr.Lloyd Jones said that Roberts was invited to go to the police station through the medium of his uncle, "subject always to the interpretation was properly carried out."

"Having got there," said Lloyd Jones, "he apparently liked being there. He was not detained at all, and he left with reluctance having been there for some days for the purpose of the inquiries. He showed no dislike of being there, and after a certain time was not kept there against his will."

The prosecuting counsel said that there was a statement made at considerable length with questions and answers on January 13, and two interviews on January 18. No pressure was brought to bear on Roberts in order to elicit any confession. Anything he had said to Superintendent Spooner of Scotland Yard were volunteered by him so far as they were able to understand him.

The Judge commented it was not that often one saw considerable statements in the form of questions and answers.

Lloyd Jones : "It was an interrogation conducted in circumstances of extraordinary difficulty."

Mr.Justice Devlin :"But what you are saying in this case is that the man was a guest of the police?"

Lloyd Jones :"He was an unusual man. He was told to go several times but stayed."

Mr.Justice Devlin :"An unwelcome guest. In fact, I shall say no more. It may be that it will have to be considered elsewhere if civil rights have been infringed."

Lloyd Jones protested that Roberts had not been kept in a cell at all, but had stayed in an upstairs room.

After the judge had directed the jury to return a verdict of Not Guilty, he discharged Roberts. As Roberts was taken from the dock to be freed, his solicitor, Mr. Myer Cohen turned to him from the barristers' bench and gave him the "thumbs up" sign, which Roberts acknowledged with a grin.

The police did not pursue the investigation into the murder of Elizabeth Thomas; Chief Superintendent Spooner returned to the obscurity of the Big Smoke with his nose slightly out of joint, glad to be rid of a case where communication barriers proved to be too tough for him. No other person was arrested or charged with the murder, which still remains unsolved.

10 : 1975 Bradford, Yorkshire

PROSTITUTED TO KILL

It was nearly midnight on Thursday 28 August 1975 when a taxi was hailed by a panic-stricken woman near Cornwall Place in Bradford, and directed to go to Sloane Square East. The driver of the cab took one look at the dirty, dishevelled state of the woman and made sure that she had the fare first before he took her where she requested to go. He observed that she was also blood-splattered and assumed that she was a prostitute who had either been in a fight or had been beaten up. He was not surprised, because the vicinity of Manningham Lane, where the woman was picked up, was famous for its concentration of prostitutes plying their trade.   (The acclaimed 1995 TV series, *Band of Gold*, was based on the prostitution activities of Manningham Lane.)

On arrival at Sloane Square East, the cab driver watched as the woman dashed to a house and hammered on the door to be let in. The door was opened by a middle-aged Black man who took one look at her, and sighed before letting her in.   He was, he supposed, one of the few friends that she had in the city and sometimes allowed her sanctuary in his house.

He assumed, as had the taxi driver, that the woman had once again been beaten up or been involved in a fight. It would not be the first time this had happened to her.

Meanwhile, back in the vicinity of Cornwall Place nearby Manningham Lane, a motorist found a man staggering round, and called out an ambulance. He was found by the ambulance crew to have been stabbed, and he was rushed to Bradford Royal Infirmary where he died at 12.15 a.m. A post mortem determined as the cause of death a single stab wound found in the dead man's chest which had severed an important artery and penetrated one and half inches into the lung.

The police investigation led by the head of Bradford CID, Detective Chief Superintendent Jack Dibb identified the dead man as Joseph Kerr-Morgan, aged 52, who lived at Otley Road, Menston but who had been staying for some time at 6 Cornwall Place, which was cordoned off along with parts of Cornwall Road when blood was discovered on the road.

On questioning witnesses, detectives learnt that there had been a disturbance in one of the houses in Cornwall Place earlier that night, and that a woman had been seen getting into a taxi. A canvass of the city's taxi drivers soon brought forward the driver involved, and information given by the driver led police to the house in Sloane Square East that the woman had been seen going into.

When the Black man answered his door for the second time that night, he was somehow not all that surprised to find police officers outside for he had guessed that whatever the woman had been up to was more serious than he had first thought. The woman was still in his house, smoking incessantly and shaking nervously, making poor attempts to clean herself up, and he had not been able to make much sense of what she was saying.

When the police officers attempted to speak to the woman, the Black man interrupted, "She's deaf and dumb."

The police officers gave each other questioning looks, before one of them produced a notebook and wrote something down.

The note read : "A man has been stabbed, he has since died." It went on to read that the woman did not have to say anything but if she did, it could be used in evidence.

"Do you understand?", the officer asked her several times, speaking slowly. The woman nodded her head.

She was then asked to come down to the police station, and led outside to a waiting panda car.

Police officers searching the house after her arrest discovered a blood-stained knife on top of a wardrobe, and bagged it for forensic examination. At the police station, the woman's blood-stained clothes were also taken away for forensic examination and she was given some custodial garments, a cup of tea, and everyone settled down to wait until a sign language interpreter was rooted out of bed and brought to the police station to assist in interviews.

On Saturday 30 August, Jean Teale, aged 28, of Sloane Square East, Whetley Hill, Bradford, appeared before magistrates in Bradford City Court charged with the murder of Joseph Kerr-Morgan, aged 52. The proceedings were interpreted by the principal social worker for the deaf in Bradford as defending solicitor Martin Read asked for reporting restrictions to be lifted and appealed for witnesses to come forward. The accused was remanded in custody pending further enquiries.

Jean Teale was the second of four children, three girls and one boy, born to a brutal father and a timid mother in a poor area of Bradford. Diagnosed when a baby as born Deaf (as was her brother, Tony - the other two girls, Joyce and Lily were hearing), she suffered a miserable childhood. Her parents would argue over her deafness, and had no patience with her if she wanted their attention. Her father left home for good before Jean got into her teens, leaving her mother to bring up the three girls and little boy.

The deaf school she went to in Bradford did not allow use of sign language, and the growing girl became extremely frustrated communication-wise, frequently being disciplined for using sign language to other children in class. She would return home from school frustrated and angry, anger which she took out on her mother. She also began to rebel and started experimenting with smoking with other children in the school toilets or playground to alleviate her frustration. The only bright spot in Jean Teale's childhood was her ability in swimming, winning races in competitions. Her feat in winning two gold medals in the Deaf Swimming championships were trumpeted in the local newspaper, the Bradford Telegraph and Argus. This article was later to be shown in court at her trial to demonstrate how far she had fallen from being a bright prospect.

By the time Jean left school, she had no academic qualifications and a low expectation of life. She started work in a clothing factory. She was quite a pretty girl, and soon began to attract the attention of boys but proved to be very naive in her relationships and social graces. She met her first boyfriend at a fair. They had only been out a few times when he took her to his home after a drinking session.

On arrival at his home, he left Jean in the kitchen while he went to the toilet to relief his bursting bladder, and whilst he was relieving himself out of the room, his brother came in and made advances to Jean, pinning her against the kitchen top and french-kissing her In her naivety, Jean assumed this was a normal thing to do and she responded enthusiastically. When her boyfriend returned to the room from the toilet, he went ballistic as he caught his girlfriend and brother kissing, and in the fight between the brothers that ensued, the kissing brother was stabbed fatally and when Jean tried to intervene between them, she was slashed across the face resulting in a scar which marked her for the rest of her life, losing her attractiveness.

In the downward spiral that followed, Jean Teale fell out with her mother over a man, with whom she started living, and became pregnant. Whilst carrying the child, the man she was living with was arrested by police for his part in a burglary. The baby, a girl, was born whilst he was still in prison, and was taken away by Jean's mother and elder sister who felt that Jean was not responsible enough to bring it up, nor give it a settled home.

Jean resumed living with her boyfriend on his release from prison, and drifted into casual prostitution to keep them both in drink.

When she became pregnant again with her second daughter, her mother arranged with a doctor at the hospital for her to be sterilised so that she could not have any more children, signing forms of consent for this to happen. Despite her sister Joyce's attempts to explain the process to her, Jean Teale had no idea or understanding of what was happening to her.

Out of hospital again, Jean met up with a pimp named David Brown, and married him in a cheap ceremony, much to the disapproval of her mother, who died shortly afterwards, and other family members. Brown then forced her into regular prostitution as her pimp, but soon got tired of her because of difficulties in communication, and took up with another woman. After a fight with Brown, in which a knife and razor were used, she left him and obtained a divorce.

Now a regular prostitute walking the streets, she got badly beaten up by a punter in a motel room while they were having sex, and was left for dead.

She was lucky to recover from that beating, but the downward spiral continued with her taking drugs and having heavy drinking sessions, which were financed by her prostitution. She also took up with a number of men, most of whom also lived off her earnings as a prostitute.

Now and then, the social workers for the deaf come across her in hospital or in the streets, but every time they attempted to persuade her to come to the deaf centre, she refused. The one rock in her life, her sister Joyce, gave her up as hopeless when she saw how filthy and abused she was, with no home to call her own.

That was how the situation was when the events of 26th August happened.

Earlier that day, the pimp Jean was then living with at 14 Cornwall Place, a Charles Callaghan, brought home another prostitute, Ann Bryce, whom he had started living with away from Cornwall Place, and had sex with her, causing Jean to become jealous and angry. She flew at the other prostitute with her fists but the other woman was bigger and stronger, and Jean lost the fight, retiring to sulk in a corner of the room with a bloodied nose while the other two continued to have sex, ignoring her presence and simmering jealousy.

Later, two other men, later named as Joseph Kerr-Morgan and Daniel Murphy, came into the flat, and all of them, together with a Thomas Elston who also lived at 14 Cornwall Place - with Jean tagging along behind - went out to the Belle Vue public house which they left at 10.30 p.m. and returned to Cornwall Place where they all drank themselves silly on cider.

Callaghan, Bryce and Elston left when they had run out of cider, leaving the other two men and Jean to sleep off their drunken stupor.

Sometime later, one of the men (Joseph Morgan) awoke from his drunken stupor and started to interfere with Jean, who pushed him off and told him to get out of the house. The two of them staggered down to the hallway where a struggle then took place, with Morgan slapping Jean in the face.

Flashbacks of her previous beating in the motel room which had left her almost dead came to Jean, and she panicked, lashing out with a knife which she carried in her handbag for protection. Freeing herself of Morgan, she stumbled out of the house and ran to get the taxi which took her to the house in Sloane Square East where she was later arrested.

Jean Teale had not known until the police officers came to the Sloane Square East house that the man she had struggled with had been fatally stabbed when she panicked with her knife, and the unfortunate woman now found herself right at the foot of the downward spiral that had started when she was a little girl, charged with murder.

On 20th November 1975, Jean Teale was committed to trial at Leeds Crown Court. This took place on 19th January 1976 before Mr. Justice Thesiger when she pleaded not guilty to the charge of murder brought by the prosecution.

David Savill, prosecuting Q.C., described to the court the events of that fateful night of 28th August the previous year. Joseph Kerr-Morgan, he said, was a strange character of contradiction who was a well-respected trade union official who would sometimes get an overwhelming craving for alcohol. During these periods, he would opt out of his normal life for days, weeks or even months and had on the 19th of June that summer left his home in Otley Road, Menton and taken lodgings at 6 Cornwall

Place, and during the weeks that followed, he had got on well with other people in the house although he was drinking a great deal. No-one, however, had complaints about him.

"On August 28", the prosecuting counsel continued, "Kerr-Morgan was seen by the witness Thomas Elston in the Belle Vue public house in the company of Jean Teale, who had been deaf and dumb since birth, and who had become a prostitute. Mr.Elston knew both, but knew of no evidence of any association between them. Later, a group which included Elston, Kerr-Morgan, a man named Daniel Murphy, Teale's pimp Callaghan and his latest lover, Ann Byrne, went to Callaghan's flat where a great deal of cider was drunk."

"The party returned to the Belle Vue and finally left about 10.30 p.m. and went back to Callaghan's flat. There was no evidence of unpleasantness or hostility. Later, three of the party left, leaving Kerr-Morgan, Teale and Murphy in the flat. Murphy was out to the world, drunkenly asleep on a bed."

"At about 11.30, Thomas Elston came out of 7 Cornwall Place and saw Kerr-Morgan in the street with blood on his chest and his shirt soaked with blood. Kerr-Morgan made some light-hearted facetious remark which shows how drunk he was, and Elston saw Mrs.Teale running down Cornwall Place towards Manningham Lane where she caught a taxi. Meanwhile, Kerr-Morgan had staggered out of Cornwall Place into Cornwall Road then into Manningham Lane where a passing motorist saw him collapse."

Mr.Savill alleged that, when interviewed by police, Teale had said :"He hit my face and pushed me," and asked why she had stabbed him, she allegedly said: "Because he attacked me."

91

Called to the witness stand, Jean Teale through a sign language interpreter said Kerr-Morgan had been one of six people drinking cider in a flat in Cornwall Place. She left the flat after telling Kerr-Morgan to get out because he was bothering her and he was drunk. He had followed her out and grabbed her, smacking her face. In answer to Geoffrey Baker, defence counsel, Teale said she had stabbed Kerr-Morgan because she was frightened. She had been carrying a knife because she was afraid of another man with whom she had previously lived.

In response, David Savill, Q.C., challenged Teale that she was hysterical "in a hopeless rage and completely distraught" that night when she saw the man with whom she had been living having sex with another woman and go with her to a party. He suggested Kerr-Morgan had slapped her across her face to bring her to her senses, not because he had been refused sex by her. Kerr-Morgan might be a strange man but not one likely to assault a deaf and dumb woman for no reason at all.

In his closing speech, the prosecuting counsel told the jury that : "If somebody was entitled to draw a deadly and lethal weapon and plunge it into a chest because of a slap across the face, that would be quite absurd, indefensible and contrary to common sense." He went on to say that the question of self-defence could not be seriously considered.

Geoffrey Baker, defending, told the jury :"Miss Teale lives in a grim, twilight world: hearing nothing - a blank wall of silence. This grim twilight world, she has not chosen. Perhaps the other world which she has lived in, she has chosen - a world somewhere between cruelty and carnality. Because of her very infirmity and disability, she has been used and ill-used, struck, beaten and punched by all the bullies and drunkards that her life inevitably leads her to meet."

He went on to say there was no evidence that Teale felt any hatred or ill-feeling towards Kerr-Morgan. She was just defending herself from a drunken man who has seized her, smacked her and started to abuse her, not letting her go. She thought she would stab him a little bit - not a lot, just little enough to make him let go so that she could flee, which she did. She had not meant to kill him. Producing a copy of the newspaper cutting from the Bradford Telegraph and Argus of 14 years previous, Mr.Baker said :"The decline in this girl has been startling. At 15, she was an attractive girl, cheerful, sunny and athletic but has since gone steadily downhill and now finds herself in this dreadful situation."

In social work reports read out to the court, Teale was said to have been involved with many men, some of whom had lived off her immoral earnings. She had often been forced out onto the streets, and frequently been badly beaten up.

In his summing up to the jury, Mr. Justice Thesiger reminded them that Teale had already admitted the stabbing, but what they had to decide was whether she was guilty of murder.

After some deliberation, the jury returned to announce that they had unanimously found the accused not guilty of murder, but guilty of manslaughter. The court was then told that Joseph Kerr-Morgan had numerous criminal convictions, some for serious assault.

In sentencing Jean Teale, Mr. Justice Thesiger said that he accepted Teale was frightened for herself in view of previous beatings which she had endured, but it was the court's duty to discourage violence, particularly with the use of a knife.

"However, I pass a sentence that is lenient, although I think in some ways, having regard to the sort of life she has had to lead recently, imprisonment is not such a disaster for her."

Jean Teale was sentenced to two years' imprisonment on 21 January 1976, which due to the length of time already spent in custody plus remission for good behaviour meant that she was released at the end of 1976.

Unfortunately, on release, she returned to her old life of prostitution and drink.

DEATH AT THE HANDS OF A CLIENT

It is often said that Deaf people are the subjects of social services 'from the cradle to the grave'. In many instances this is an undeniable fact. A file is opened on a Deaf person from the moment of his/her birth or the moment it becomes deaf and comes to the attention of the social services agency, and is never closed until the person dies. For long periods, the file may lie dormant but it is nonetheless there, and will be retrieved and added to every time the subject has need of social work assistance, often for such mundane matters as having been in receipt of environmental aids such as a flashing doorbell or a baby alarm system. The file is never destroyed, and will only go into the 'dead files' or be destroyed when it is stamped 'Deceased' across the front of the folder. Because of this, many Deaf people have a love-hate relationship with their social workers, who often face an unenviable task when dealing with their clients because of external pressures imposed upon them. These pressures may be due to financial reasons, or due to rules and regulations set out by their employing authority which state the parameters within which they should function.

An additional pressure may well be that the social worker's sign language communication skills are not "good enough" for a Deaf British Sign Language user. Whatever the reason, it is not often that a social worker is able to resolve an issue to the complete satisfaction of a Deaf client, especially where the client does not fully understand (or wish to understand) the reasons why the issue could not be resolved completely to his or her satisfaction.

However, Deaf people do not go round killing their social workers!

So, when a blood-splattered man walked into a Southampton police station on 4 July 1978 with a note which said: 'I have killed Mr.Gray', the shock and horror reverberated throughout the Deaf Community and social services personnel who work with that client group.

Quickly determining the man was emotionally disturbed and Deaf, the police placed a call to the social work offices. The call was taken by Canon R.G.Young, a chaplain for the Deaf also employed in a social work capacity, who went to assist the police. (It was common in those days for some clergymen to have worked with Deaf people as 'Missioners' before the local government reorganisation in 1974 resulted in social work agencies being established employing qualified and trained social workers. Many 'Missioners' transferred duties they had previously been carrying out to social work agencies before being phrased out or retiring.)

With information gleaned through the interpretation by Canon Young, the police went to a house in Warren Avenue in the Shirley area of Southampton, where they found the body of Peter Gray, a social worker based in the Woolston Area social services office in Southampton. He had been subjected to a 'frenzied' knife attack.

James Alexander Gray, who preferred to be known as Peter, was aged 48 at the time of his death, and had come to social work after 22 years in the Royal Navy. He took his C.Q.S.W. at the Polytechnic of North London and became interested in the deaf when he spent a month on placement at the Royal School for Deaf Children in Edgbaston, Birmingham. After a period as a generic social worker with Hampshire Social Services, he returned to the Polytechnic of North London to undertake the

Certificate of Social Workers with the Deaf which he completed between 1975 and 1976. During that period, he worked on placements in the Royal National Institute for the Deaf's rehabilitation centre at Court Grange, Newton Abbott, in the Alban Association for the Deaf in Hertfordshire, and at the psychiatric unit for the deaf at Whittingham Hospital, Preston.

On 4th July 1978, an unemployed Deaf labourer named Jeffrey Gregson, aged 37, of Coxford Road, Southampton, appeared before the city's magistrates court charged with the murder of James Alexander Gray and was remanded in custody until 18th July pending further police enquiries.

The accused, Jeffrey Gregson, had been educated at the Royal School for Deaf Children, in Margate, Kent, and had an history of aggressive behaviour due mainly to frustration. He was not helped by his inability to communicate effectively with his family. On one occasion, he had come home from the Margate school for the holidays, to find that his parents had disappeared, and young Jeffrey had to be cared for by the police and social services whilst his parents were traced.

Upon leaving school, he became an apprentice joiner, being described as 'one of the best', but was unable to hold down a permanent job. He was often dismissed from his employment for aggressive behaviour, which included throwing things at other employees. This may have been a result of taunting, but is more likely to have been frustration caused by imagined 'slights'.

He married a girl he met in Portsmouth Deaf Club, and they quickly had a baby daughter. However, his marriage was more often off than on due to his aggressiveness. Even so, he and his wife had three more daughters, two of them twins. He badly wanted a son, and this contributed to his sense of frustration and failure, especially when allied to his inability to hold down a job due to his behaviour.

On the day preceding the murder of Peter Gray, his mother had been found dead at the foot of the stairs at her home in Warren Avenue, Shirley, and Gregson had been particularly distraught over her death. Although her death was later recorded as an accident due to a fall down the stairs, there had been some suspicion that Gregson had pushed her down the stairs in a domestic argument, and Canon Young, with whom Gregson got along particularly well, had been out to see him and console him over his loss.

Canon Young was preparing to go and see him again, when Peter Gray called and told him that he was going out to Shirley to see Gregson, so Canon Young said he would be out later. One hour later, the police telephoned to advise of Peter Gray's death.

No-one really knows for sure what happened on that day of 3rd July when Peter Gray met Jeffrey Gregson at his mother's house. It was clear, however, that Gregson was both emotionally and mentally disturbed at the time due to his mother's death. In Gregson's head, there was also a growing list of people both known and unknown who Gregson believed were trying to kill him, and it was possible Gregson had included Peter Gray on that list of people trying to kill him.

The point has also to be said that Peter Gray's sign language skills were very iffy, due to not having worked for long with deaf people. They were inadequate for use with a person who was very agitated. Difficulties in communication may therefore have contributed to Gregson's feeling of grief and frustration and led him to explode and attack his social worker with a kitchen knife which was recovered from the scene of the murder.

The trial of Jeffrey Gregson took place at Winchester Crown Court on 18th December 1978 before Mr. Justice Willis. The accused pleaded 'not guilty' through a sign language interpreter to the charge of murder, but 'guilty' to manslaughter. The plea was accepted.

Speaking at the trial, the Director of Hampshire Social Services, Arthur Hunt, said that the killing of Peter Gray was a tragic reminder of the dangers often faced by his staff.

"Mr.Gray was a very brave and extremely committed man who had been highly regarded by his colleagues," said Mr.Hunt. "His death is being felt very keenly. This case was a particularly difficult and complex one, but it does underline the very real risks faced by staff, particularly in the field work, when often they are dealing with disturbed people."

In accepting the accused's plea of guilty to manslaughter, Mr. Justice Willis said :"Your actions have led to the death of a particularly brave and dedicated social worker whose life was devoted to helping the deaf and dumb."

He ordered that Jeffrey Gregson be detained 'without limitation of time' at Park Lane Hospital in Liverpool, a special high-security establishment for the criminally insane.

Gregson remained in this establishment for a number of years before being released in the late 1980's, and lived a solitary life in Southampton before dying in 1995 aged 55 years.

Peter Gray's widow, Barbara, set up a trust fund in memory of her husband for the benefit of social workers who wished to increase their skills for working with those who were deaf or whose hearing was impaired.

12 : 1981, Saltcoats, Scotland

THE WITNESS WHO LIED

Years of sexual debauchery, peddling of pornographic pictures, allegations of an incestuous relationship between mother and daughter, and of child abuse through neglect, inflamed through alcohol abuse into intense jealousy boiled over in the early morning hours of 26th October 1981 when an angry and abusive man stormed up to a group of revellers dancing away the night in a packed Amanda's Discotheque in Irvine, a small town on the west coast of Scotland near Ayr.

Yvonne Sinclair, aged 36 and profoundly Deaf, was taken aback by the anger of William Mair, who was also Deaf, who was demanding in sign language where his two children were.

"You've left them all alone while you go out and have a good time!"

Mrs.Sinclair had been minding Mair's two children at her home while he had gone with other members of the Saltcoats Deaf Club to play in a pool tournament being held in Ayr Deaf Centre, and as far as she was concerned, they were still safe at her home.

It was evident, however, that Mair was so drunk and argumentative and being restrained with some difficulty by his friend Alex McLeish that Mrs.Sinclair decided it would be best if they all left Amanda's and returned to her house in Howat Crescent, Irvine to avoid a rowdy scene at the discotheque.

En route to her house, Alex McLeish admitted to Mrs.Sinclair that Mair had been argumentative and drinking all afternoon in Ayr Deaf Centre, at one stage running out of money and having to be subbed by McLeish for more drink.

On arrival at Mrs.Sinclair's home, the situation with Mair was made worse by the discovery that Mair's youngest son, also named William, was found to be bleeding from a cut head which he said he got by running round in the house and falling over against a table. While Mrs.Sinclair bathed the wound and put a dressing on it, Mair ranted and raved accusing the woman of neglecting his children while she partied the night away at the discotheque. The row grew worse when Mrs.Sinclair hit back and taunted Mair about his sexual prowess.

"You can't get it up and you have a small dick!" she screamed at him.

Before the row could escalate into violence, Mrs.Sinclair managed to manhandle Mair with some difficulty out of her house through the door, helped by McLeish, who then drove Mair home with his two sons.

Shortly afterwards, Mrs.Sinclair's daughter Helen, aged 17, arrived home at 2 a.m. from a night out accompanied by her boyfriend, Anthony Wilson who had been locked out of his own house nearby. Wilson asked to stay the night and after chatting to Mrs.Sinclair, they both went to bed in Helen's room.

A little later, however, Mrs.Sinclair came up into Helen's bedroom and asked Helen to join her in her own bed, and Wilson drifted off to sleep.

It seemed that he had been asleep only minutes when someone opened the door, switching the lights on and poking his head around the door. The lights were switched off almost immediately and Wilson tried to get back to sleep but was further disturbed by a racket which included radiators being banged, doors slammed, raised voices including a cry of "Tony! Help!" which he ignored.

There were also sounds of someone leaving the house, and a car starting up.

Wilson had learnt that Deaf people tended to be very noisy without realising it, and he ignored everything. Eventually, all quietened down and he was able to drop off to sleep properly again.

The next morning, however, he was woken up by a scream and Ian, the 12-year old son of Mrs.Sinclair running into the bedroom shouting "Murder!" Jumping out of bed hurriedly, he found parts of the house covered in blood, and in one of the downstairs rooms, there was the naked body of his girlfriend lying in a pool of blood. She had been badly battered.

In the next room lay the mother, also covered in blood. Police and a nearby doctor neighbour were called immediately.

Both Yvonne and Helen Sinclair were still alive, but very badly injured, and the women were rushed unconscious by ambulance to Kilmarnock Infirmary, where it was decided because of the extreme severity of the injuries and the inadequate facilities of the local hospital to transfer them both to a specialist neurosurgical unit at the Southern General Hospital in Glasgow where surgeons fought to save their lives.

However, Helen Sinclair died later that evening without regaining consciousness, while the mother remained in a critical but stable condition in the intensive care unit.

Detectives questioning neighbours and Tony Wilson soon uncovered details of the argument at the discotheque the previous night, and the fracas in the doorway of the Sinclair home when William Mair was evicted from the house.

William Mair was later arrested that night at his home in Griffen Road, Saltcoats and taken to Kilmarnock police station where he was charged with two counts of serious assault.

Later that night when it became known Helen Sinclair had died, the charges were changed to include the murder of Helen Sinclair and the attempted murder of Yvonne Sinclair.

Making an appearance in Kilmarnock Sheriff Court the next day, he made no plea of declaration and was remanded in custody pending further police enquiries, and subsequently ordered by Sheriff A.V.Sheehan to stand trial at the High Court in Glasgow the following February.

At the trial, Dr.Ruth Ritchie giving evidence stated that she was a neighbour of the Sinclairs and had been one of the first called to the house to help the women. She had found it very difficult to recognise Helen Sinclair because of the nature of the injuries and the blood which covered her face and hair. "There was blood everywhere, on the bedding, the carpets, the walls and the radiators," she said. It was obvious a terrific struggle had taken place in the house.

The senior casualty officer who had been on duty at Kilmarnock Infirmary when the two women had been brought in, Dr.Daniel McSorley, stated that when he had ascertained the nature of the two women's injuries, he had made the decision to have them transferred to the Southern General Hospital in Glasgow because the injuries were so serious. He had not been surprised to learn Helen Sinclair did not recover, and thought that Yvonne Sinclair had been very fortunate to survive.

The court heard details of the post-mortem from Professor William Harland who had carried it out. He stated that there were at least four separate blows of "great violence and tremendous force" caused by a heavy, blunt instrument in a frenzied attack which had smashed the victim's skull like an eggshell. The cause of the death of Helen Sinclair were due to skull fracture and cerebral abrasions as a consequence of the assault.

It was alleged in court that after being evicted from Mrs.Sinclair's house and taken home by Alex McLeish, resentment over his treatment by Mrs.Sinclair had festered in Mair so much that he had returned to the Sinclair home armed with an iron bar, still angry at what had happened earlier. He had searched the house, disturbing Anthony Wilson, and had battered the two women unconscious. Wilson was criticised for ignoring what was going on.

Alex McLeish, through a sign language interpreter, described the events of the day and night of 25th and 26th October. The Saltcoats Deaf Club had a game to play in a pool tournament being held in Ayr Deaf Centre, and he had driven Mair with his two sons to Yvonne Sinclair's house to be minded during the day. After dropping off the two boys, he had picked up another player, and the three men had gone to Ayr in his car. He stated that Mair got involved in an argument in Ayr with another man over a point of issue about a pool match, and had started drinking heavily, subsequently running out of money. He admitted loaning Mair more money to buy drink because Mair was in an angry mood, and he had not wanted Mair to cause trouble.

When they had returned to Irvine after the pool tournament and dropped off the third man, they had gone to Mrs.Sinclair's house but had found the lights out and Mair had lost his temper at the thought of his two sons being left alone. Matters grew worse when Mair found out that Yvonne Sinclair was partying the night away at Amanda's discotheque and McLeish had taken Mair there because Mair wanted to have it out with the woman.

Then, when back at the Sinclair house, there was a terrific row over the cut on young William Mair's head, which Mair blamed on Yvonne Sinclair's neglect. McLeish confirmed that during the argument, Yvonne Sinclair had taunted and rubbish-ed Mair on his sexual performances, which had inflamed the situation even more. He had difficulty in getting Mair out of her house and getting him home with his two sons who were frightened at the sight of their angry father.

After dropping off Mair and the two boys, he had then gone on to his own home and had not realised until the next day that Mair had returned to the Sinclair home.

Asked by Donald Macaulay, Q.C. for the defence, about the relationship between Mair and Sinclair, the witness stated that as far as he was aware, they had known each other for eight or nine years, and it was fairly well known that Mair sometimes stayed the night with Mrs. Sinclair while her husband was away working in Japan. He could not say if they were having a sexual relationship, although there was a presumption that they were.

Pressed by Mr. Macaulay, McLeish had to admit he had handled a number of compromising pornographic photographs of Mair and other deaf people which had been taken by Mrs. Sinclair during "parties" at her house. These "parties" had been of a sexual nature, and the photographs had in some cases been quite explicit. He had given some photographs to Mair in the toilets of the deaf club. They were contained in an envelope which he had told Mair to hide.

Called to the witness stand, Yvonne Sinclair claimed that the events of the night of 25/26th October were a "complete blank" to her. She could not remember what had happened, and strenuously denied having a sexual relationship with Mair while her husband was away in Japan.

The witness admitted under Mr.Macaulay's questioning she had a Polaroid camera and liked taking photographs as a hobby, but denied taking compromising pornographic photographs of several deaf people including Mair in her house, and handing them round in the deaf club.

However, there was a dramatic twist two days later when Yvonne Sinclair was branded a liar in court. Recalled to the witness stand, she was forced to admit that the statements she had made on oath earlier in the trial had not been true. The previous night, she had been made to go by her husband with him to the police station in Irvine, and tell them that she had been telling the court untruths.

Mrs.Sinclair was warned by the judge that perjury was a very serious offence.

She told the court the reason for her lies was because she had been "frightened of her husband as she had never told him of her sexual activities and did not want him to find out she had a relationship with Mair."

Asked by Mr.Macaulay if she had been having sex with Mair for as long as seven years, she denied this, saying that it had only been for three or four years. She told the court that Mair often stayed over at her former house in Middlepart Crescent, Saltcoats on Tuesday nights after the deaf club had closed for the night because it was nearer to his place of work. She insisted the relationship had been over for about a year before the incidents at her house in Irvine due to her relocation, but was forced to admit she had recently left a note with the gateman at Mair's place of work signed "Love, Yvonne".

Mrs.Sinclair also admitted that Mair was not the only man who occasionally stayed overnight in her home while her husband was away.

Mr.Macaulay also had the witness admit to "sex parties" at her house where she had taken pornographic photographs of other deaf people, and that these photographs had been circulated in Saltcoats Deaf Club. Asked by Mr.Macaulay to enlarge on the relationship of sleeping with her daughter when her husband was away in Japan, she insisted that this had just been "for company", and this had been the case on the night of 25/26th October. She could not explain why her daughter had been naked when found by her son and Wilson.

Branded a liar and shaken by her experiences under questioning, Mrs.Sinclair was stood down with her reputation in tatters following the evidence of her sexual practices.

Anthony Wilson, in giving evidence, broke down in court when he relived the moment he had found his girlfriend's body, and was visibly upset in court when he identified a photograph of her. He stated that although he had pretended to be asleep when someone had come into Helen's bedroom and switched the light on, he thought he had recognised Mair as the intruder.

Giving evidence in his own defence in sign language, Mair admitted he had returned to the Sinclair house after being evicted and taken home by Alex McLeish. He said he had been in a blind rage, and waited until McLeish left for his own home before taking a crowbar and returning to Howat Crescent, using the crowbar to break into the house.

He had gone to Yvonne Sinclair's bedroom intending only to punch her or beat her up, but had panicked when someone had woken up, and he had hit out with the iron bar several times without thought.

It was only after he had gone into the bathroom where he was sick, and had switched on the lights that he realised to his horror that Helen had been in bed with her mother, and that she had borne the brunt of his frenzied attack.

He said he had never meant to harm Helen whom he had liked, and described how he had carried her to another room to try and make her more comfortable. He could not say why he had also brought Yvonne Sinclair down the stairs. He denied that he had gone to the Sinclair house with murder on his mind, but agreed he had been drinking heavily.

Mair said he then ran away from the Sinclair home in a panic but was arrested by the police a few hours later. He had been shocked when he learned that Helen was dead.

In summing up, the judge asked the jury to remember that it was Mair who was on trial, not Yvonne Sinclair, and no matter how unsatisfactory a witness she was and how much they disapproved of her lies and evidence of sexual practices, it was their responsibility to look at the facts in a clear manner to decide on the case against Mair.

William Alexander Mair was found guilty of the murder of Helen Sinclair, and the attempted murder of Yvonne Sinclair. He was told that he had deliberately set out to "cause harm", and was sentenced to a term of life imprisonment.

13 : 1985 Llanfairfechan, North Wales

STAMPED TO DEATH

When Mrs Wendy Williams noticed on the morning of Saturday 20th April 1985 that the front door of one of her neighbours' house was partly open, she thought nothing of it.

The occupant, 60-year old Gwyn Jones of 4 Greenfield Terrace, Llanfairfechan in North Wales had a reputation in the small, coastal resort as a heavy drinker, frequenting the many public houses in the village, and Mrs.Williams just assumed that he had been so drunk the night before and had forgotten to close his door.

She did not know him well, but had often heard him making his way home from the pub in the early hours of the morning, mostly at weekends. He had a habit of causing a racket dancing and singing in the street, often shouting out in particular to other neighbours, "Goodnight Mrs.Roberts, Goodnight Mr.Roberts!"

The previous night, however, the rowdiness had been louder than usual, and there had also been the sound of shuffles and running feet, and she felt a bit resentful of Gwyn Jones for disturbing her.

"Let him sleep off his drink," she thought, resentfully

When a friend, Anthony Webb, called at lunchtime to see if Gwyn Jones wanted to go with him for a drink, the front door was still open, and the milk and newspaper still had not been taken in. Pushing open the door to let himself in, the friend was shocked to find Gwyn Jones lying in the hallway of his house, one side of his face bashed in as if with an iron bar. Webb immediately left to call the police.

The first police officers on the scene found that the resident of the house was dead. There was evidence that a struggle had taken place in the hallway which was badly splattered with blood. Gwyn Jones had suffered severe head and facial injuries, including a clear imprint of a heel on the face which indicated he had been stamped on with some force.

On making initial house-to-house enquiries, police soon elicited the fact that Jones had a liking for drink, and that the public house he most frequented was the Pen-y-Bryn Hotel in Llanfairfechan, where he was often seen propping up the bar.

Mr.David Roberts, licensee of the Pen-y-Bryn, confirmed that Gwyn Jones had been in his bar the previous night and had been drinking up to closing time at 12.30 a.m. when he left to go home.

There had been a disco held in the hotel that night, and police soon learnt that there had been an argument at one stage during the evening between the deceased and a younger man.   The argument had flared up on two separate occasions, and was due to Gwyn Jones' habit of poking fun at people when drunk. The younger man had objected to Jones's manner.

The second time the argument had flared up happened in the toilets which had resulted in a minor scuffle between the two men. However, Jones had been gone at least 10 minutes before the other man had left the hotel at 12.40 a.m. The landlord was clear about this point as it was when the washing up was being done, and the hotel being made ready for business the next day.

When asked to identify this younger man, the licensee and his wife said that he was a deaf person with poor speech from Anglesey who sometimes stayed with his sister at weekends in Mount Road, Llanfairfechan. He was named as Neville Roberts.

Later that evening, Neville Roberts was seen at his sister's house and requested to accompany police officers to police headquarters at Bangor. At the same time, several articles of clothing stained with what looked like blood were taken away for examination.

In the police car taking him to Bangor, Roberts was told that Gwyn Jones was dead, and he broke down and cried. At Bangor police headquarters, he made a statement agreeing that he had a fight with Gwyn Jones who had been taunting him and making fun of his poor speech all evening, but he had not killed him.

However, forensic evidence taken from his clothing, particularly his shoes, showed that Roberts had been the person who had fought with Gwyn Jones and left him for dead. He was committed at the next magistrates court for trial at Caernarfon Crown Court.

Neville Parry Roberts was aged 23, and worked in a factory in Newborough, Anglesey where he had lived with his father. A former pupil of the Royal Cross School, Preston, Neville Roberts had suffered a miserable childhood with a physically and emotionally abusive father. His sister stated at the trial that she encouraged him to come and stay with her and her husband at Llanfairfechan at weekends to get him away from their father who constantly taunted him about his deafness.

But it was on the fateful visit to Llanfairfechan in April that the events leading up to the murder unravelled.

In his opening speech at Caernarfon Crown Court on Wednesday 13th November 1985, Alex Carlisle, Queen's Counsel for the prosecution, told how the accused had festered a resentment all evening after the victim had taunted him and called him names, and made fun of his deafness. Mr.Carlisle also told how this resentment had led to the accused following the victim home and assaulting him in his own house. The court was told that the injuries received by the victim indicated he had been repeatedly kicked "as if he was a football". The victim had also been stamped by the accused's heel so hard and so often that his face had flattened out, and there was a clear heel-print imprinted on the face. All this had happened while the victim had lain supine on the floor of his hallway. It was, said the prosecution, an attack of totally unwarranted severity and violence out of all proportion to the argument which had gone on earlier between the two men.

In his defence, Neville Roberts denied the charge of murder. He said that he had gone to stay with his sister, as he often did, to get away from his brutal and abusive father, and had gone to the Pen-y-Bryn for a few drinks. He had not known there would be a disco on, but he had stayed nonetheless.

Through his sign language interpreter, the accused said he had first noticed Gwyn Jones, whom he knew by sight, staring at him and making comments to other people about him, pointing his finger at him. Roberts said he was sensitive to other people poking fun at his deafness, as his father had, but had at that stage tried to ignore the deceased.

Later, when he was in the hotel toilets making a stand-up discharge, he had felt a shove on his back which caused his head to bang on the wall of the urinal, and his urine to splash down his trousers. Roberts said this had made him angry and he had spun around and asked Gwyn Jones what he had done that for, and received in response a load of verbal abuse, all that he could understand being the words "fuck off".

"It shocked me," Roberts signed to the court. "I thought he was mad. He was walking strangely, as if drunk, so I walked away."

The accused denied that he had waited until closing time to follow Gwyn Jones out of the public house so that he could go to his home and murder him, as alleged by the prosecution. Although he had been annoyed by Gwyn Jones and his aggressive attitude, he had put it down to him being drunk, and he had not wanted any trouble.

In any case, Roberts stated, Jones had been gone from the pub for at least ten minutes before he himself left the pub, as confirmed by the licensee. However, Roberts found that Gwyn Jones was still outside the pub when he had come out, as if he has been waiting for Roberts. The deceased had then subjected Roberts to renewed verbal abuse, followed by a punch to the eye. Jones had then staggered off to his home.

"I did not follow him on purpose," Roberts told the court in rebuttal of the prosecution's allegations, "but my sister's house was in the same direction, so I preferred to let him go on ahead before I followed to avoid further trouble. I wanted him to get home first."

Roberts said he had to pass Gwyn Jones's house to get to his sister's house. Jones was still outside when Roberts arrived on the scene, and he had actually walked past Jones when he turned round just to make sure that Jones was not doing anything as he could not hear, and observed the victim mouthing off and gesturing obscenely at him.

"I said to him, 'why don't you fucking shut your mouth and get inside home', but he continued to taunt me so I walked over to the old man. I got hold of him. I was pushing and pulling him, shaking him because he was pointing his finger at me. I was upset and I had enough of him, this swearing at me, pushing me in the toilets, messing my trousers, pointing his finger a me. I just had enough."

Roberts admitted he had got mad and angry with Jones. He felt that what he had been subjected to all evening was exactly the same as his father had behaved when he was physically abusive. He had struggled with the old man, and they both fell through the doorway into the victim's house. Jones had elbowed him in the stomach, and this made him more annoyed. "I wanted to hit him, bruise him and his face to be swollen, that's all. I wanted to give him some hurt but I did not want to kill him, no way."

Roberts stated he had hit Mr.Jones about five times that he could remember, and had then left the house to go home, leaving him lying on the floor. Roberts said he believed that Jones was just hurt and still alive, but when he arrived at his sister's house and saw the blood on his clothes and his shoes, he became frightened and when his sister started to question him about what had happened, he had lied to her, telling her he had a fight with two boys on the way home from the pub.

It was only after his arrest the next day, and in the police car on his way to Bangor police headquarters that he learned that Gwyn Jones was dead and he had broken down and cried.

Counsel for the Defence, John Rodgers, told the jury that at worse, it was a case of manslaughter, not premeditated murder. Gwyn Jones's habit of getting drunk and making fun of people might appear harmless, but it was a real irritant and very provocative to some people who were sensitive to this sort of thing, as Roberts was due to his unhappy childhood suffering from physical and mental abuse, and also because he was handicapped by deafness and poor speech. He made a plea for mercy and urged the jury not to go for a murder verdict, but one of manslaughter.

However, Alex Carlisle for the prosecution told the jury in his closing speech that not all deaf people went round attacking those who provoked them, and that whatever Mr.Jones had said or done to the accused that night, it did not justify the severity of the extremely violent response that had been the end result.

He reminded the jury that the post mortem showed there had been at least 20 very hard kicks to the face and the body, as well as stamping on the face with a heel. The victim had seven broken ribs, and a squashed face but death had resulted from asphyxia caused by a fracture of the larynx, probably caused by a very hard stamping of the heel on the throat or neck. There was no indication whatsoever, notwithstanding the defendant's claim to have been hit in the eye and elbowed in the stomach, that the victim had attempted to defend himself.

The jury of seven men and five women were out for just over an hour, and one of the women jurors wiped away some tears as the "Guilty" verdict was read out to the court.

There was disbelief and sobbing from women and other relatives and friends of Roberts in the public gallery who did not feel he justified a murder charge, but one of manslaughter as Mr.Justice Leonard told Roberts : "The jury has found you guilty of murder for which there is only one sentence in law. It is that you will serve a life imprisonment."

As Neville Parry Roberts was led away to begin his life sentence, the judge told the jury he agreed fully with their verdict, despite protests from family members and friends who immediately sought ways whereby an appeal could be made against what they felt to be an unfair trial.

An appeal was accordingly launched against the verdict on the grounds that the defence failed to call a psychiatrist to give evidence on the problems of deafness, and to testify that Neville Roberts' abuse by his father plus communication difficulties, compounded by alcohol could have contributed significantly to the loss of self-control. Instead, the defence had made do with a report presented to the court by the psychiatrist.

Heard at the Court of Criminal Appeal before Lord Justice Watkins, and Justices Tudor Evans and Auld on 25th July 1989, counsel for Neville Roberts made the submission that this failure to call the psychiatrist amounted to a miscarriage of justice.

However, It was held by the Appeal Judges that the trial judge, Mr. Justice Leonard, had made the jury fully aware of the appellant's disabilities and characteristics in his summing up. Indeed, the judge had highlighted these and had concurred with the defence's decision not to call psychiatric evidence, stating that this medical evidence would not have added any further enlightenment to what the jury already knew of the facts of the case.

The appeal was dismissed.

14 : 1986 Newton Abbott, Devon

A MINOR ARGUMENT

Throughout the country, there are establishments specifically set up for the rehabilitation of all types of people with learning difficulties, behavioural problems, or socially disadvantaged. There are such establishments for Deaf people as well.

The country's largest national organisation for deaf people, the Royal National Institution for Deaf People (R.N.I.D.) operates such a centre in the village of Abbotskerswell, near Newton Abbott in Devon.

A former Sunshine Home for Blind Babies, Court Grange was purchased by the R.N.I.D. in 1962. Set in 11 acres of grounds, the establishment consisted of a 19th-century large house with an unique turreted roof, with extensions.

In 1986, although called a school by outsiders, it was a social and vocational training centre for severely hearing-impaired young men who were also educationally, emotionally, vocationally and/or socially disadvantaged. Although it did not take in any who required confinement for corrective training, it did take in young Deaf men with a history of delinquency - provided admission was of their own free choice and not the result of a court or custodial order.

Those who attended Court Grange were therefore not called 'inmates', as they might have been in a custodial establishment, or 'residents', as they might have been in a care establishment, but 'trainees' as the whole purpose of their two or three year stay in Court Grange was to help them to develop life and employment skills to enable them to become independent and employable in open or sheltered employment after their stay.

Like any other establishment where people are thrown together in close proximity, friendships may be formed between individuals which is encouraged as part of social life skills training. On the other hand, conflicts and personality clashes may also occur, especially between young people who may have in their home environment had behavioural problems which demanded attention, attention which in Court Grange had to be shared with other people.

On the evening of 22 April 1986, such a conflict arose between two trainees during the showing of a video in the lounge. It appeared to be a minor matter which led to 'words' being signed at each other in violent and obscene terms, and was quickly resolved by a staff member present in the room.

Later in the night, however, around 11.15 p.m., there were sounds of a commotion upstairs, and the staff member went up - he thought - to deal with a fight, and realised with shock when he got to the landing that it was more serious than he thought.

On the floor of the landing lay a 18-year old young Deaf man without speech named Matthew Lewis, who originated from Reading in Berkshire who had been in Court Grange less than a year, and was well-liked in the training centre.

He was lying in a pool of blood, and standing nearby holding a bloodstained knife was another Deaf trainee named Paul Espie, who was 22 years old and one of the older trainees in the centre.

They were the same two young men who had earlier had the minor altercation in the lounge during the showing of the video.

With the help of other trainees, the staff member disarmed Espie, and placed him in secure accommodation before going to call the ambulance and the police.

The victim was pronounced dead and the body removed for a post-mortem which determined that he had suffered three knife wounds to the heart, three into the left lung and another most violent injury on the top of the right shoulder which had also penetrated the lung.

Espie was taken into custody upon arrival of the police and told them through one of the staff translating from sign language that : "It was an accident. It was a fist fight, and I took the knife from my belt."

Matthew Lewis' parents were notified of the sad news at their home in Reading, and travelled to Newton Abbott the next morning to formally identify their son's body.

Paul Espie appeared before Teignmouth Magistrates Court on Thursday 24 April accused of the murder of Matthew Lewis, and had the proceedings interpreted for him by Michael Adair, senior social worker with Deaf people with Devon County Council. He was remanded in custody, and eventually on 15 July 1986, indicted for trial at Exeter Crown Court.

Bob Clowes, principal at Court Grange, issued a statement to the Press in which he said that both young men, who were friends, were popular, co-operative and doing well on their training courses. He stated that everyone at Court Grange shared the shock and grief experienced by the families of Matthew Lewis and Paul Espie.

On Monday 17th November 1986, the trial of Paul Espie took place before Exeter Crown Court. The presiding judge was Mr. Justice Smith-Stuart, and the proceedings were fully interpreted.

The accused pleaded not guilty to a charge of murder but guilty to manslaughter by virtue of diminished responsibility. His plea was accepted by the court.

Prosecuting counsel, Paul Chadd, Q.C., told the court that the stabbing of Matthew Lewis has taken place on 22 April at Court Grange, Abbotskerswell. Three days earlier, Paul Espie had gone into Newton Abbott to do some shopping, and had purchased a knife, and concealing it, had smuggled it into Court Grange.

It was not known why the accused had purchased the knife.

Mr.Chadd described to the court the events of the evening of 22 April, and told how the accused's deaf friends at the training centre had very responsibly assisted staff in disarming Espie, and looking after him until the arrival of the police to arrest him. Then through their own sign language, they were able to give full and clear statements through interpreters to the police.

Defence counsel, Neil Butterfield, Q.C., produced four medical reports on Espie before the court, and said : "I say nothing about the offence. This is a tragic young man imprisoned within the walls of his own profound deafness."

Consultant psychiatrist Dr. John Philips told the court that Paul Espie was suffering from a mental illness. Without treatment, his condition would deteriorate but treatment might alleviate his condition.

After hearing that a bed would be made available within 28 days at Rampton Hospital, a top security mental hospital in Nottinghamshire, Mr. Justice Stuart-Smith committed Espie to the hospital, with a restriction order without limit as to the time he should stay there.

In another Press statement, Bob Clowes stated : "The cause of this bizarre tragedy was the onset of a mental illness to a young man who also happened to be deaf. This distressing tragedy and the court's findings confirm that deafness confers no immunity from mental illness."

The statement added : "Since that time (of the incident), the support and encouragement from families of trainees, professionals and particularly local people has been very much appreciated. It has enabled the valuable work of the centre in preparing deaf people for independent living and for competitive employment to continue."

Court Grange is still in existence, but in moving with the times, now calls itself a college.

15 : 1988 Newport, South Wales

THE CASE OF THE FOUR TRIALS

The start of the weekend, and Tony Wesson cheerfully waved goodbye to his mother as he left to go the short distance to a flat at Tewkesbury Walk in Newport, Gwent, a town about 15 miles from Cardiff, the capital city of Wales. The date was Friday 1st July 1988.

Flat number 9 Tewkesbury Walk was where Tony Wesson's fiancee, 20-year old unemployed Suzanne Greenhill, had lived since moving there from a hostel for single homeless teenagers almost two years previously. Wesson had helped to decorate the flat, and had often stayed there at weekends and he had his own key to the place.

Parking his car shortly before 6 p.m. in the spaces provided for occupants of the flats complex, Wesson observed that the curtains and blinds were drawn closed, which was unusual for the time of the day. Taking out his set of keys, he unlocked the main entrance to the flats complex then went up the stairs to the front door of the flat, unlocking that as well to enter the flat.

He was shocked to find the flat in some disorder, the patio door open, and going into the main bedroom, he found Suzanne lying in a pool of blood on the floor. Touching her, he found the body to be cold.

Alerted by Wesson's frantic pounding on their door, neighbours Hazel King and Ernest Morgan alerted the police.

The call was logged at Newport Central police station just after 6 p.m., and the first officers were on the scene shortly afterwards, along with paramedics from the ambulance service.

The first detectives on the scene noted the body was lying on her right side with a substantial amount of blood in the immediate area. A strip of plaster had been placed across her eyes in the form of a blindfold, and the victim's own panties had been stuffed into her mouth.

After police surgeon Dr. Clason-Thomas had pronounced life extinct, Scene of Crime specialists went through the flat carefully, taking body tapings and vaginal swabs as evidence. A footprint was also found on the floor of the bathroom, and photographed as further evidence.

Initial questioning of Tony Wesson alerted the police to potential problems for the murder investigation. The victim had been Deaf without speech since birth, and Wesson was himself also Deaf, and it became quickly apparent that the couple were very active within the local Deaf community with a large circle of Deaf friends whose first language or main means of communication was British Sign Language, and none of the current officers in the Gwent Constabulary were knowledgeable in that language.

It was therefore imperative that sign language interpreters be quickly brought in.

In the meantime, the body of Suzanne Greenhill was removed for a post-mortem to be performed by a Home Office pathologist, Dr.Kellett, who revealed that death was due to multiple stab wounds. The post-mortem also provided evidence to suggest that the victim had been raped after she had been stabbed, as a small amount of chafing to the vagina had been observed, and the vaginal swabs had shown human semen to be present. Although DNA profiling was unable to be carried out due to the low sperm count, blood grouping was successful and revealed that the semen originated from a male who was a "O" non-secretor.

As the finder of the body, Tony Wesson had to be the first suspect and under police questioning, he revealed that he had last seen his fiancee on the Tuesday of that week, 28th June, when he had taken her to his home where they had tea.

After their meal, they had driven to the home of some mutual friends, Anthony Roberts and Bernadette Miller, who lived together, but had only stayed there a few minutes before going on to Newport Leisure Centre with the intention of doing some weightlifting in the fitness room which contained a multi-gym.

Already in the fitness room was a cousin of Suzanne, Sean Lewis, who was surprised to see her there as he was a regular and had not seen her there before.

"We had a shower afterwards," Wesson continued, "then left about 9.30 and called at John's to return a catalogue."

John turned out to be another mutual friend called John Wilkinson, who confirmed that the pair had stayed a few minutes, and after embracing and saying goodbye outside his home, they had separated, Suzanne walking the three-quarter mile distance to her home carrying her sports bag.

From that point onwards, Suzanne's movements were not known until Wesson discovered her body three days later, and it became crucial for the police to fill in this gap.

A task force of 40 police officers headed by Detective Chief Superintendent Waters, with Detective Chief Inspector Glynn as second-in-command, was set up to deal with the murder enquiry. For DCI Glynn, the situation was slightly personal and ironic as he lived ten doors away from the Greenhill family, and whilst he had not known Suzanne that well, he did know her mother, Wendy Lesley Greenhill, her step-father and younger brother quite well, and additionally, Lesley Greenhill's sister (Suzanne's aunt) was married to a police sergeant.

The task force faced a number of difficulties. Aside from the fact mentioned earlier that both the victim and her fiancé were Deaf, there was also the clue of the open patio door and no sign of any break-in at the flat. This indicated that the murderer may have been known to the victim and in that case would almost certainly be another member of the local Deaf community, although - perhaps to confuse the issue - the police released the possibility that Suzanne Greenhill had left the patio door open while she had gone to look for her cat outside, and some stranger had slipped in behind her and had surprised her when she came back in, with or without the cat, of which there had certainly been no sign at the scene of crime.

Other difficulties concerned the length of time the body had lain in the bedroom, and the need to ascertain the precise whereabouts of the deceased between 9.30 p.m. on Tuesday 28th June, and Friday 6 p.m. 1st July. The difficulties in this particular area were immense, not the least due to a number of alleged sightings made of the victim on the Wednesday and Thursday, 29th and 30th June in response to newspaper appeals by the police, made by a number of people who would normally be reliable. These included other Deaf people who should have been familiar with her, as well as neighbours and a postmistress at the local post office where Suzanne usually cashed her unemployment Giro. The last alleged sighting of Suzanne had been at 7.05 p.m. on the Thursday evening, 30th June but this did not tie in with the scientific facts produced by the post-mortem which showed that due to the decomposition that had set in, Suzanne had been dead at least 36 hours before she had been found.

The last complication or difficulty was that the murder had happened during the week of the Newport Carnival and a travelling fair had been in the town. The possibility still had to be borne in mind that Suzanne had been murdered by a stranger, and that this stranger might have had some connection with the fairground people.

In order to resolve the uncertainty over the time of death, a second post-mortem was carried out by Professor Knight on behalf of the Gwent Coroner, and the professor subsequently produced a statement that read "having regard to all aspects it is not inconsistent that death could have occurred three days prior to the body being found." In other words, it was clear the killing could possibly have happened the evening Suzanne returned home from the Newport Leisure Centre.

Evidence from the scene of crime tended to support the theory the murder had happened on the Tuesday night, and not on the Wednesday or the Thursday, despite the alleged sightings of Suzanne on those days. Most important, perhaps, was the fact that she was still wearing the same clothes she had worn that evening, although to be sure, these clothes had been disarranged. The description of these clothes was confirmed by Anthony Roberts, Bernadette Miller, Sean Lewis and John Wilkinson, who had all seen and spoken to Suzanne on that Tuesday night. In addition, her sports bag which she had taken to the leisure centre was still on the kitchen top unopened next to her set of house keys. As she had showered at the leisure centre, the bag included her wet towel and sweaty sportswear she had worn, items that she would have been unlikely to have left in her bag but taken out to be washed at the earliest opportunity.

The police were therefore looking at the probability that on entering her flat after walking home from her goodbye embrace with Tony Wesson outside John Wilkinson's house, Suzanne had gone straight into the kitchen and deposited her sports bag and keys on the kitchen worktop before being surprised by someone who was already in the house, who had maybe already intruded through the patio door. Alternatively, she had either met the murderer on her way in and let him in, and he had exited through the patio doors to avoid being seen.

To pursue this viewpoint, however, it meant the police task force had to regard all alleged sightings of Suzanne on the Wednesday and Thursday as being those of mistaken identities or incorrect due to dates and sightings being mixed up. To further confuse matters, Suzanne had dyed her blonde hair burgundy red only that Tuesday but all publicity photographs circulated by the local press or carried on television showed Suzanne in her original blonde hair and no-one had commented on the colour of the hair when making the alleged sightings.

As police began to undertake their investigation into the murder in earnest, details of the life of Suzanne Greenhill began to surface.

Born deaf, her parents separated when she was six weeks old, and her mother re-married when she was aged three. From the age of four onwards, Suzanne had attended a succession of special schools in Gwent and in South Glamorgan, the last being the Ashgrove Special School for Deaf Children in Penarth, where she had been a residential pupil, and which she left when she was aged 17 with no academic qualifications. Her mother found that the school residency had made her quite independent, and arguments followed within the family with Suzanne rebelling against restrictions which were being placed upon her, so when she became 18, Suzanne left home and resided in a hostel for the single homeless in Newport where she thrived on her renewed independence. Her living away from home caused her relationships with her mother and stepfather to improve.

After she had met Tony Wesson, Suzanne moved into Flat no.9 at the Tewkesbury Walk complex in Newport, where several other Deaf people, including Tony's partially-deaf sister Amanda, and others with physical or learning difficulties also resided.

It was also clear that despite her engagement to Wesson, Suzanne was not above dispensing sexual favours to other men, including other Deaf men. To quote one police officer, "she was oversexed".

Even Tony Wesson admitted during questioning that although he had enjoyed a healthy sex life with Suzanne, she had put ever increasing demands upon him which he was unable to meet, and had purchased a sex toy (a vibrator) a month before the murder to assist with the sexual demands she was placing upon him.

This line of investigation opened up other possibilities, and threw up a number of other suspects.

One strong suspect was an ex-boyfriend of Suzanne called Glen Dempsey who had taken offence when Suzanne and Wesson started going out together, and had waylaid Wesson one evening at the hostel for. the single homeless and given him a beating, causing Wesson a broken nose and a fractured cheekbone. It had been this beating that had been the deciding factor in Suzanne moving out of the hostel into 9 Tewkesbury Walk.

Another possible suspect was Timothy Robson, who had been found by Wesson inside the victim's flat a number of times, and who had once taken ages to answer the flashing doorbell of his house when his mother-in-law had called to visit. Suzanne Greenhill was found to be in the

The Pen-y Bryn, scene of the fight that led to murder. (Chapter 13)

Court Grange College. (Chapter 14)

Cafe Customers being questioned by detectives. (Chapter 15)

The Suzanne Greenhill billboard. (Chapter 15)

Timothy Robson playing snooker. He missed a match on the night of the murder. (Chapter 15)

Suzanne Greenhill enjoying a joke at Newport Deaf Club. (Chapter 15)

house, sitting on the settee with her tee-shirt inside out, as if having had to put it on in a hurry.

On 2nd July, there was a flurry of excitement when police were called to a house in Croesycelliog, Cwmbran following reports that a man assisting in the murder enquiry had taken an overdose, and taken to hospital, where he was pronounced dead.

Wyn Ffrancon Davies, aged 37, was a social worker with Gwent Social Services with special responsibility for services to Deaf people, and was in fact caseworker for Tony and Amanda Wesson, and had been at Tewkesbury Walk assisting police as an interpreter in interviewing Amanda, plus other Deaf people less than 24 hours earlier.

However, police ruled out any link with the murder of Suzanne Greenhill and called his death a tragic coincidence.

In a statement to the media, DCS Mark Waters stated "Mr.Davies' death does not form part of our enquiries. We were very happy with his assistance. He was a professional, dedicated and caring person and very concerned that something like this had happened in the Deaf community. His death is very tragic, and we have every sympathy with his family and friends."

Friends and colleagues of the social worker said that he had been suffering from pressures due to stress-related work problems.

In another press conference, DCS Waters announced that the police had found a bloodstained item which was thought to be the murder weapon but refused to enlarge further on the topic. He also confirmed that Suzanne had been sexually assaulted during the murder.

As the days rolled into weeks, and the weeks into months, the Suzanne Greenhill murder enquiry became one of the longest murder hunts undertaken by Gwent police. Some 4,700 people were interviewed during the seven-month enquiry, more than 2,700 lines of action were followed up, and over 500 statements were taken.

The murder hunt was notable for a number of 'firsts'. A total of ten sign language interpreters were used by police as they sought to build up knowledge of the lifestyle of the victim, and this task was to take them into the heart of the Deaf community all over the country.

It was also decided to appeal to the BBC's *Crimewatch* programme to feature the murder hunt, and DCI Glynn was deputised to present the case on the programme.

Then, horror of horrors!

Crimewatch was one of those programmes which had been deemed unsuitable to be close-captioned for teletext subtitles for deaf and hard-of-hearing people. Neither did the programme have a minicom line for deaf or hard-of-hearing viewers to telephone in any responses.

An embarrassed BBC subsequently subtitled *Crimewatch* for the transmission of this murder enquiry, and installed a minicom line. Not a programme has been missed being subtitled since, and the minicom call line is a permanent fixture.

The transmission on *Crimewatch* produced over 200 responses which all had to be followed up by the murder squad.

Interest in the case was revived at the beginning of February when a police spokesperson announced the arrest of a man for the murder of Suzanne Greenhill. They refused to comment further other than to state that the man was still "helping with inquiries" but reporters noted that sign language interpreters were accessing the police station where the suspect was being held, and deducted that the he was a member of the Deaf community. Magistrates twice granted police permission to extend time for questioning.

On the morning of Monday 8th February 1989, Timothy Jack Robson appeared in Newport Magistrates Court accused of the murder of Suzanne Greenhill, and was remanded in custody.

The events which led to this arrest had started with a conference of the murder squad, now reduced to ten from the original forty officers, to review the investigation. Part of the review looked at the way the police had been interviewing Deaf people, and deducting their answers given in response to questions. It was advice received from professionals working with deaf people, including the then headmaster of Ashgrove School for Deaf Children, that the police had possibly been making incorrect deductions from the verbal translations by sign language interpreters of the interviews they had had with Deaf people that decided them to draw up a list of people to re-interview. At the top of their list of people to be interviewed was Timothy Robson and his wife Tracey.

The answers previously given by Robson had never been satisfactory, and he had been a prime suspect in the murder almost from the beginning of the investigation. Indeed, many of his colleagues at his place of work, Montague Meyer, a local timber merchant, and people who frequented the same clubs which Robson also frequented, had also very strong suspicions of his involvement with the murder.

For one thing, he had been seen with scram type marks on his face immediately after the time the murder had been committed, and he had also been seen with a bandage around his right hand. One of his friends had even said to him, "You killed her because she wouldn't let you fuck her!" to which Robson had replied angry, "You're crazy. Don't be fucking stupid!"

However, police had never been able to get any incriminating statement from Robson's wife, Tracey, and while she continued to support Robson, he remained nothing more than a very strong suspect whilst police attempted to obtain evidence from other sources which would incriminate him.

Their chance of breaching Tracey Robson's support of her husband came in January 1989 after her divorce decree absolute had come through. Tracey had left Robson in the July of the previous year, just after the murder, and had filed for divorce on the 20th July on the grounds of cruelty and unreasonable behaviour.

Towards the end of January, therefore, police had determined to re-interview Tracey Robson. Although she was partially deaf, it was decided to use a sign language interpreter, social worker Margaret Roberts, to assist in the interview, during which she was asked again for her version of the events of Tuesday evening the 28th June 1988, the time which police were now convinced Suzanne Greenhill had been murdered. All "sightings" of Suzanne on the Wednesday and Thursday 29th and 30th June were now being dismissed by police as "mistaken". Another woman had been mistaken by witnesses for Suzanne, and other witnesses had confused the dates and times they had thought they had seen the victim.

Under questioning, Tracey Robson now stated that on the evening of 28th June, her ex-husband had left home at around 7 p.m. wearing his "V" necked jumper in the red of Wales, with the Welsh feathers embroidered on it, carrying his snooker case. He had stated he was going to meet up with "Dave", whom she thought to be a friend she knew, at the Gaer Club where he usually played snooker and was team captain, then go into Newport town centre.

He had returned home at approximately 11.30 p.m. the same night, and put down the snooker case and taken off his jacket. She had noticed immediately that he was shaking, and appeared angry. His hand was swollen and his knuckles were red, and he had three scratches on his face which she believed were caused by fingernails. She also noticed that the accused had blood over his jumper, shirt and trousers. There was also blood on the inside of his trainers and over the toes.

He had told her he had a fight with a man in a pub in Newport over an argument about a girl who had scrammed him, and asked her not to tell the police, his mother or her mother.

Timothy Robson had then stripped down to his vest and underpants, and taken his outer clothing into the kitchen. She had heard the washing machine being switched on, and her husband walking upstairs. Tracey had then gone into the kitchen, and noticed that the washing machine was set at No.11, for a quick wash, and made tea when her husband came back downstairs and got the clothes out of the washing machine, namely the red jumper, shirt, trousers and socks.

Before retiring to bed, she had seen him putting his trainers by the side of the gas fire to dry out, and the next morning, he had scrubbed them in the kitchen sink before replacing them by the gas fire to dry out again.

The coming weekend, after the body of Suzanne Greenhill had been discovered, she had gone to her mother and related the story of the previous Tuesday night to her.

Based on the statement of Tracey Robson, police officers led by Detective Sergeant Webber and accompanied by an interpreter, Hugh Jobson, arrested Timothy Robson at

7.45 a.m. on Wednesday 1st February 1989. The arrest took place in the street outside his house at 126 Gaer Park Drive as soon as Robson had stepped outside to go to see his parents up the street at no.147 as was his custom before going to his place of work at Montague Meyer. He was taken to Newport Central police station where he was detained for questioning, and it was 8 p.m. that night before his mother was informed by police officers that her son had been arrested and charged with the murder of Suzanne Greenhill.

A search warrant was then applied for, and the accused's home was searched by forensic experts and other police officers, which resulted in evidence directly connected with the murder being found. These included the red "V"-necked jumper found in a wardrobe in the front bedroom, which witnesses stated Robson had been in the habit of wearing to the Gaer Club for snooker matches, and which they had never seen him wear for some months, since the murder in fact.

His parents home at 147 Gaer Park Drive was also subject to a search warrant, and other items of evidence recovered from both houses included a set of keys found in a locked cash box in the same wardrobe where the red jumper had been found, a copy of the South Wales Argus dated 13th July 1988 with an article concerning the murder, and a large number of photographs which indicated the accused had a fetish for women's breasts. The photographs included cuttings from pornographic magazines, and undeveloped films which revealed Robson had taken them off pornographic videos which he had stopped using the pause button on his television.

The keys were positively identified as those which had gone missing from Suzanne Greenhill's flat about two years previously, and fitted the airing cupboard and closet in the flat. Missing from the set of keys were those which opened the communal door to the flats, and the entrance door to the flat itself. These keys became significant when a witness came forward to state that sometime during the summer of 1987, Robson had showed her a set of keys which he said were for the flat of Suzanne Greenhill, and which she had given to him so that he could periodically check on her well-being.

The photographs were significant for the police in view of the fact that after she had been stabbed, the victim's tee-shirt and bra had been lifted up and the breasts exposed for viewing.

Police also recovered from the house nine pairs of ladies' knickers which did not belong to Tracey Robson who stated that it was not unusual for her to find other women's knickers hidden by Robson in their house.

Other finds of significance for the investigating officers included a "ghoul" type face mask and a record sleeve which showed a creature like a ghoul standing over the body of a woman who had been killed with a knife which was dripping in blood. The dead woman had a black strip across her eyes. It will be remembered that Suzanne Greenhill, when found, had a strip of plaster stuck across her eyes and she had also been stabbed, so this pointed to a possible motive that Robson had been acting out a fantasy when he allegedly killed Suzanne.

Finally, police also found a book on infertility which had been purchased around the time Robson and his wife were trying for a baby. The couple had in fact seen a consultant obstetrician at the Royal Gwent Hospital in Newport, submitting a semen sample which showed Robson's sperm count was so low that he was almost certainly infertile. This tied in with the semen found in the vaginal swabs taken from Suzanne's body which had proved to be so low that DNA profiling was not possible.

During the lengthy questioning of the suspect at Newport Central police station, Robson continually denied having been at 9 Tewkesbury Walk on the night of 28th June, denied having sex with Suzanne, and denied having murdered her, denied having blood on his clothes or washing them or his trainers, sticking resolutely to his alibi of having been in a fight and accusing his ex-wife of lying to try to get him into trouble. Asked why he had arrived home breathing heavily and perspiring, he responded that sometimes he ran home.

Initially, Robson stated that he received the cut to his face when he had been pushed into a beer glass during an argument in a Newport public house, and persisted with this story for the first two days of questioning, during which time he was also fingerprinted, had his feet printed, and had blood samples taken. The footprint sample was found to match that which had been photographed from the bathroom floor in the deceased's house, and the blood sample confirmed that Robson was a "O"-type non-secretor, consistent with the semen samples taken from the vaginal swabs.

On the resumption of questioning by DS Webber on the morning of Friday 3rd February, Robson asked at 10.15 a.m. for a consultation with his solicitor, Dudley Harmston, in private and it was not until 4.15 p.m. the same day that police questioning could proceed.

In this interview, Robson stated that his earlier story had not been true, the reason being that he had got into a fight and thought he would get into trouble.

His alibi this time was that he had left home the Tuesday evening in question, at approximately 7 p.m. as confirmed by his ex-wife, and had gone to a public house in the town centre called the Sovereign Bar, where he had chatted up a girl at around 9 to 9.30 p.m. when a man approached and pushed him away. This man had been joined by two other men in a threatening manner, and he had become frightened and ran out of the pub, chased by the three men through the streets of the town, past the bus station and the Royal Gwent Hospital alternatively walking and running, until the three men caught up with him at a spot on Cardiff Road adjacent to Belle Vue Park where he was punched and fell against the perimeter of the wall, and the abrasions to his face had been caused by the rough surfaces of that wall. He had sustained his hand injury punching one of his attackers before escaping into the park by climbing onto the roof of a bus shelter.

Robson confirmed that he had left home with his snooker case, and arrived back there still with it. He insisted he had carried it through the chase, the fight and the scaling of the bus shelter!

At the first hearing in the Magistrates Court, Robson's solicitor Dudley Harmston asked that reporting instructions be lifted and made an appeal through the media for witnesses to come forward and confirm the alibi of the accused.

No-one ever came forward to provide evidence of the fight or to support the story. The fight was even denied by the barmen on duty at the Sovereign Bar that Tuesday night. They stated that there had been no disturbances whatsoever that night, or indeed for the whole of that week, in the Sovereign and they remembered the period well because it was the time of the Newport Carnival and had culminated with the discovery of the body of Suzanne Greenhill.

However, if the police thought the case was over, they were in for a nasty surprise for it was an incredible three years before Robson was finally to be convicted, after four trials and two appeals!

The trial of Timothy Robson, a carpenter of Gaer Park Drive, Newport, opened before Mr.Justice Roche on Tuesday 3rd October 1989 at Cardiff Crown Court with Philip Price, Q.C., as prosecuting counsel. A team of sign language interpreters were booked to provide interpretation from the initial charge being put, through to the judge's summing up and the verdict because many of the 80 witnesses were themselves Deaf.

Timothy Robson entered a plea of "Not Guilty" to the charge of murder.

In his opening address, Patrick Price described how neighbours had found Tony Wesson cradling his head in his arms and howling after finding his fiancee's body lying in a pool of blood in her flat. Blood marks on the door had led Mr.Wesson to a scene of horror where the stabbings had taken place. It was, he said, a frenzied knife attack resulting in six separate blows to the neck and throat, severing the carotid artery and spraying blood everywhere. There had additionally been one in the back which had been delivered with considerable force. Besides being partly naked and having her panties stuffed down her throat, the victim was also blindfolded with adhesive tape "cutting off a principal sense which was left to her" (meaning that she was without means of communication).

The court heard that she had been dead for a considerable time when found, and there was clear evidence she had been forced to have sexual intercourse against her will. The prosecution alleged that the murder took place on the night of the 28th June 1988.

Mr.Price referred to forensic evidence which would show that semen taken from vaginal swabs were identical to

Robson's, and that red fibres which had been recovered on body tapings matched a red acrylic sweater known to have been worn regularly by Robson and which he was allegedly wearing on that night, and which had not been seen until it was recovered from a wardrobe in his house.

Suddenly, on the fifth day of the trial, Mr.Justice Roche stopped proceedings and dismissed the jury with no official reason being given. This had apparently been because one of the jurors had been making unauthorised comments about photographs of the body of Suzanne Greenhill, and it would have been unsafe for the trial to proceed.

The trial was then re-opened with a new jury on the following day, but was held up at the end of October to allow for talks between the accused, counsel and the judge and no evidence was heard for several days.

Then, on the 2nd of November, all of Robson's defence team quit the case, forcing the judge to discharge the jury for a second time, again with no official reason being given.

Behind the scenes, however, it was known that new, improved techniques in DNA profiling were now available, and the prosecution would say that the new tests would prove conclusively that the semen found in the vaginal swabs came from Robson, who continued to deny involvement in the murder.

Mr.Justice Roche granted an application for a new trial, which began on 29th January 1990.

The highlight of the third trial was the evidence presented by Tracey Robson, ex-wife of the accused, who described the events of the night of 28th June one and half years previously when her ex-husband had returned home saying he had been in a fight, and how he had taken his clothes off straightaway and had put them in the washing machine, something he had never done before, and the next day had scrubbed his trainers with a nail brush.

Central to the defence case was the series of alleged sightings of Suzanne after the Tuesday the prosecution stated she had been murdered. A number of witnesses offered evidence of the sightings, including a sighting by a friend of Suzanne's named Jenny Vincent who said they had talked with each other on the Wednesday, but these were dismissed as mistaken sightings, and the jury found Robson guilty of murder.

He was sentenced to life imprisonment, still denying the murder.

Sensationally, on 13th March 1992, the conviction was overturned by the Court of Appeal in London which ruled the conviction was "unsafe and unsatisfactory " because of material irregularities late in the third trial which were unfair to the defence. Lord Justice Taylor said that the judge should have discharged the jury, and his legal directions to the jury were open to criticism. The Law Lords ordered that a re-trial take place.

The fourth trial of Timothy Jack Robson took place on 9th July 1992, and is a record for the number of times an accused has stood trial for the same murder charge.

In this trial, Robson - faced by the conclusive DNA proof - admitted for the first time that he had had sexual intercourse with Suzanne, but claimed it was with her consent, and that when he had left her, she was all right, but the prosecution contended that he had lain in wait for her, and had subjected her to a sexual attack in carrying out his fantasies as demonstrated on the record sleeve.

The jury of six men and six women only needed 45 minutes in retirement in coming to an unanimous guilty verdict. As the verdict was read out in court, Robson's mother, Joan, screamed out, "Never! Never!"

The killer was then sentenced to life imprisonment for the second time, still protesting his innocence and still denying his involvement in the murder. However, the forensic evidence had been overwhelming, and his lies and prevarications regarding his alibi or movements for the night in question told against him, particularly as they could not be supported by any witness.

His parents, Cyril and Joan Robson, broke down in tears and called the verdict a great injustice, and said they were still standing by him, convinced of his innocence.

Today, as this book is written (October 1997), Joan Robson - now widowed - is still utterly convinced of her son's innocence and still actively campaigns for the re-opening of the case.

Timothy Robson himself, when seen by the author, gave exactly the same story that was disbelieved by the jury and the courts of appeal. He has never admitted to the murder.

In July 1997, Channel Four featured the murder of Suzanne Greenhill in its *Trial and Error Live* programme, and raised the possibility that Robson had been wrongly convicted, following which Joan Robson got a telephone call from a man who claimed that Robson was innocent, and that he knew the name of the real murderer of Suzanne Greenhill.

Gwent Constabulary, however, stated they were "satisfied" Robson had been rightly convicted.

Tracey Robson left Newport, and is now living under a different name with a new partner and a baby. She refused to be interviewed by the author.

The Deaf Community is still divided in Newport over the murder.

16 : 1993 Wallsend, Newcastle-upon-Tyne

STABBED TO DEATH

"I'm going to my grandmother's house," Paul Reynolds told his mother after a family row one night in April 1993, then stepped out of the house in Malvern Road, Wallsend near Newcastle, face wracked with pain.

However, he had only got a few yards around the corner into Lisle Grove before he started to stagger and collapsed onto the tarmac where he was found a few minutes later by passers-by who called an ambulance but when it delivered him to Newcastle General Hospital's casualty department, he was pronounced dead upon arrival.

The cause of death was a single stab wound just below the collarbone which penetrated the heart, and caused massive internal bleeding.

Back at the house in Malvern Road, his mother Sandra Reynolds and her common-law husband, David Hall, glared at each other angrily before their attention was drawn to the knife Hall was holding in his hand. Blood was dripping from it.

"Oh God!" Hall signed to Sandra, "I have stabbed Paul!"

Earlier that evening, the couple who were both Deaf, had been out for the evening to their local Deaf Centre where Hall, depressed because he could not find work as a carpenter, had become moody and argumentative.

The arguments between the couple continued when they arrived at their home, where they had lived together for 15 years. The relationship between David Hall and Sandra Reynolds was often stormy, with frequent rows which included violence. This time Hall raised his fists to her, hitting her on the back of the head, starting a noisy scuffle.

Paul, aged 24, who worked as a machine operator for a graphics company in Washington across the River Tyne, was making sandwiches for his supper in the kitchen when the row, followed by the fight, started. On hearing what was going on, he came out of the kitchen still carrying the knife which he had been using to prepare his food, and pulled Hall away, telling him to leave his mother alone.

Enraged, David Hall turned upon him, accusing him of taking his mother's side. Hall was also insanely jealous of his stepson because Paul had a job, whilst he was unemployed and finding it hard to find work. Pulling up his pullover and his shirt, he bared his chest to his stepson and challenged him to stick the knife into his chest.

"Come on, come on, do it! I'm fed up with my life!" Hall shouted.

"Don't be so daft!" Paul said dismissively.

Hall then said, "If it makes it easier, I'll get you a sharper knife!" and then pushed past his stepson into the kitchen, returning with a six-and-half inch sharply pointed kitchen knife and waved it at Paul. "Here, take this and stick it in me!"

Paul Reynolds shook his head and said, "No, you do it yourself!"

At that moment, Sandra Reynolds saw the knife and jumped at her common-law husband, believing that he was about to attack either herself or her son. In the struggle that followed, Paul went to her aid again to try and separate the pair and walked into the knife.

After the fight had stopped and everyone had calmed down a little, no-one had realised that Paul had been stabbed except that Paul felt pain in his chest, and decided to get out of the house to go to his grandmother's house, both for help and to get away from the atmosphere in his mother's house.

Police officers who had been called to Lisle Grove at the same time as the ambulance soon found out where the victim had lived, and went round to the house on Malvern Road where they found David Hall still with the knife, and disarmed him, taking him into custody.

At his trial at Durham Crown Court in March 1994, David Hall, aged 46, pleaded not guilty to murder. Prosecuting counsel Paul Worsley, Q.C., stated that the Crown did not believe that Hall had formed a careful plan to murder his stepson, but that it had happened in a burst of anger after a violent argument between the accused and his long-time partner, Sandra Reynolds, and that the victim had been stabbed during a fracas when protecting his mother.

Through a sign language interpreter, Hall told the court that he had never intended to harm Paul Reynolds and that the death had been accidental caused by Paul's intervention in the row between him and his mother.

Hall was cleared of murder, but was found guilty of manslaughter, and sentenced to three years in prison. In sentencing Hall, Mr.Justice Waller said that in determining the most appropriate sentence he took into account the extra pressures Hall would face in prison because of his disabilities.

The sentence of three years outraged Sandra Reynolds and her family, especially as Hall had already spent a year in custody, and for good behaviour, could be released on parole before Christmas that year.

Speaking to newspapers through a sign language interpreter after the trial, she signed angrily :"I am disgusted at the sentence. I am disgusted that the value placed upon the life of my son is only three years. Paul was a loving, quiet son who worked hard at his job, and David was very jealous of him and used to taunt him about it. He was a violent person who always said that if we ever tried to kick him out of the house, he would smash it up."

She also accused Hall of taking advantage of his deafness, and playing on the sympathy of the court by saying how difficult it would be for him in prison in order to get a lenient sentence.

17 :   1993 Sunderland

MURDER BY FIRE

"Mammy!Mammy!Mammy!"
The screams of a little girl heard over the roar of a fire horrified neighbours who had tumbled out of their homes, many still in their nightwear, shaken awake by a loud explosion from a house in Atlantis Road, Farringdon, an estate of mainly council houses to the south of Sunderland in north-east England, half an hour after midnight on the 19th of May 1993.

Some of them were galvanised into taking desperate action to try to get into the house to rescue the people inside.   Disabled neighbour, 56-year old Edward Robinson smashed windows with his walking stick whilst others tried to get inside.   They managed to batter the door open, but were all forced back by the ferocity of the flames, and watched helplessly until the arrival of the fire brigade.

"They were pitiful, dreadful cries," Robinson was to tell newspaper reporters later, "and they will haunt me all my days."

Fire-fighters wearing breathing apparatus battled their way into the house which neighbours said was occupied by Lesley Hutchinson, aged 27, and her daughter, Emma, aged 5, and found them huddled together in an upstairs bedroom, together with the family dog which was dead.

The little girl was brought out first, and taken in hand by another neighbour, John Hindmarch, who had paramedic training.

Hindmarch tried to revive her with first-aid techniques on the pavement while waiting for the arrival of an ambulance, then went with her in the ambulance to

Sunderland General Hospital where she was pronounced dead on arrival. She had been badly burnt about the face and hair. The post mortem later showed that the little girl had died from smoke inhalation.

Meanwhile, her mother was also brought out and rushed into intensive care at Newcastle General Hospital where her condition was described as critical with 35 per cent burns to her body.

After the fire had been doused, and the embers sufficiently cooled enough, police and fire brigade investigators then began the search for clues to determine the cause of the blaze which had resulted in the death of Emma Hutchinson, and badly injured her mother.

It was soon obvious from forensic evidence that investigators were looking at a case of murder by arson. Traces of petrol were discovered in several places about the burnt house.

Lesley Hutchinson, the victim in intensive care, was a profoundly Deaf woman without speech, and separated from her husband, Ronald, aged 30 and also Deaf. They had met in a deaf club in 1987 before getting married. Their only daughter, Emma, was hearing.

Ronald Hutchinson was picked up by the police and taken to Sunderland West police station where he was informed of the fire through a sign language interpreter, and questioned as to his whereabouts at the time of the arson attack. He proved to have an alibi which could be substantiated and eliminated from their enquiries.

However, the questioning of Ronald Hutchinson had provided enough information for the police to enable them to make certain enquiries about the behaviour of a suspect in the arson murder.

Nonetheless, it was a shock for neighbours when Lesley Hutchinson was arrested by senior detectives from

Sunderland as she was being discharged from Newcastle General Hospital after four weeks in the burns unit where she had skin grafts to her hands. Her stay in hospital had included 6 days on a life support machine in intensive care, where for a time, her life had been in the balance.

The shock was all the more puzzling to neighbours because she had been known to be a good and loving mother to Emma.

A sign language interpreter had accompanied the police officers to the hospital to explain to her why she was being arrested, and was also present during the lengthy questioning in the Sunderland West police station where she had been taken following her arrest.

It was a tricky time for the police because the suspect's hands had been so severely burned in the fire, and as she could not talk, they had to be sensitive as to how she communicated her answers in sign language. To ensure that all the questioning was fair, the police arranged for her interviews to be video-taped in their entirety, the first time a local police interview had been video recorded as well as put on audio tape. Two interpreters, one for the suspect and one for the police, were used throughout the interviews.

During the interviews, Lesley Hutchinson consistently denied that she had been responsible for the arson. Nonetheless, police were satisfied that they had sufficient evidence to warrant charging her with the murder of Emma Hutchinson.

However, at her trial the following July in Teesside Crown Court, it was stated that while in custody and during conversations with psychiatrists, Hutchinson did accept what had happened without actually admitting responsibility.

Police told the court that she had planned the murder-suicide so carefully that for the prompt action of the fire services would have seen two deaths instead of one, not counting the dog.

The court heard that the marriage of Ronald and Lesley Hutchinson, who had an explosive temper, had been going through a very stormy period, caused by Lesley's belief that Ronald had been having an affair with another family relative.

There was nothing to substantiate this belief and the affair had been strenuously denied by Ronald, but the depression caused by Lesley Hutchinson's beliefs caused violent rows between the pair, and following one row, her husband had walked out of the marriage and gone home to his parents.

To his parents, Ronald Hutchinson had expressed his fears and his concern for the safety of his daughter, saying that on at least two occasions, he had removed a can of petrol from his wife who seemed to be obsessed by fire and that he feared for her sanity. It was these allegations made by Ronald Hutchinson when he was subsequently questioned by the police following the fire that had led them to suspect that Lesley Hutchinson had actually gone and done what she had previously threatened to do, particularly as she had also made it clear she did not intend her husband or his parents to have custody of or to bring up her child in the event of the marriage ending.

The court was told that Hutchinson had so carefully planned to kill herself and Emma that she had moved a television set and video recorder into the garden shed with a note that the electrical goods were to be given to her family. A bag full of Emma's clothing was also put into the shed with a note indicating that they were to be given to her pregnant sister. A suicide note was also left for her husband laying the blame for the deaths on his supposed affair.

She had then walked down to a garage in nearby Durham Road with Emma where she was captured on the garage security video filling a five litre can of petrol which would later be used to set her home on fire.

She was seen by one of her neighbours later in a dazed condition, as if she was drunk, but subsequent blood tests proved inconclusive on this point.

Around midnight, Hutchinson doused parts of the house with petrol. Forensic experts were to find after the fire traces of the petrol on the lounge carpet, stairs, landing carpet and on bedding in the daughter's room.

Hutchinson was then alleged to have set fire to the house, then collected Emma and the family dog and shut herself with them in her bedroom where fire-fighters were later to find the tragic pair with the dead dog.

In evidence given to the court, it was said that even as she was being rescued, Lesley Hutchinson struggled to stop the firemen helping her, although police believed that at one time when it was too late, she had changed her mind and broken a bedroom window to attract help.

The court learnt that Emma Hutchinson was dead on arrival at Sunderland General Hospital, and that she had died of carbon monoxide poisoning and burns.

Lesley Hutchinson pleaded not guilty to murder but guilty to the manslaughter of Emma on grounds of diminished responsibility, and her defence counsel, David Robson QC, asked the sentencing judge Mr.Justice Potts to consider making a non-custodial order by putting her on probation so that she could still receive psychiatric treatment and counselling from the National Centre for Mental Health and Deafness at Prestwich, Manchester.

Mr. Justice Potts however refused to consider any sentence due, he said, to the incompetence of the probation service in not preparing a report for the court on time. He deferred sentencing for a week on the condition that she was returned to Prestwich.

The following week, 27 July 1994, Hutchinson sobbed as the judge told her through an interpreter: "What you did was totally wrong and wicked. You went and bought petrol and locked the doors in your home then set fire to it."

"I am satisfied that it was a determined attempt to take your life and that of your daughter. I am also satisfied with the medical advice which suggests that you were suffering severe depression. Your balance of mind was affected by severe stress and depression at the time."

"Prison does not cater for deaf people and I am satisfied that it would be inhumane to send you there. You no longer present a risk to the public and therefore a prison sentence would be wholly inappropriate."

Mr.Justice Potts then made a probation order on Hutchinson for three years on the condition that she spent the time at the National Centre for Mental Health and Deafness, Prestwich, where she had been an in-patient for the past year and continued to receive psychiatric treatment and counselling.

The bitter family of her estranged husband, Ronnie Hutchinson, called it a travesty of justice that she had escaped a custodial sentence.

18 :   1994 Edinburgh, Scotland

A CHILLING ECHO OF DEATH

Deaf people are spared the sound. They cannot hear it, but all those who did will always remember the echo that reverberated throughout Peffermill Court in the early hours of Thursday 6th January 1994. It was like the damp, sickening sound of a dull explosion followed by an eerie silence. This was heightened by a chill fear, heightened by the sound of wailing sirens which followed shortly afterwards.

In Peffermill Court, a 14-storey block of flats in the Craigmillar area of Edinburgh, Adrianius Vanputten on the fifth floor woke with fear in his stomach, recognising the noise from the previous September when a neighbour had thrown himself out of his flat to his death.

On the 6th floor, James Murdoch and his wife were wakened by the bang just after 2 a.m. and went to the window. Looking out, he saw a body lying on the ground.

On the ground floor, the building's security camera captured the whole event. Just as the video clock had registered 2.12 a.m., there was a white blur and when the image cleared, something white and grotesque could be seen lying on the pavement.

Along with other residents, Adrianius Vanputten called the police who were deluged with telephone calls, and a patrol car was soon on the scene. The occupants of the car noticed that the man's injuries were more than what could have reasonably been expected from a fall from a height, and reported back to headquarters that they had a suspicious death on their hands.

The patrol car crew were instructed to await arrival of detectives and to seal off the scene to preserve forensic evidence.

Detectives set up an incident caravan in the forecourt of Peffermill Court whilst forensic experts examined the body. The dead man appeared to be in his thirties or forties, and door to door inquiries were commenced inside the block of flats in an attempt to identify the body.

In Flat 1 on the 14th floor, police received no answer to their persistent knocking although a light showed underneath the door which indicated the flat had recently been used, and might even have someone awake inside.

On breaking the door down to gain entry into the flat, police found the apartment to be blood-spattered. Bank notes stained red with what looked like blood were drying on a radiator, and the occupant was sitting silently on his couch.

"I stabbed him in the stomach nine times. I am sorry. I opened the window and threw him out," he allegedly told one of the first detectives to enter the apartment, and added, "I never murdered anyone before."

A press statement issued by police to reporters later that morning confirmed that they were treating the death of a man who had plunged 150 feet as suspicious and had taken a man into custody who would appear in court the following day. They were not able at that stage to confirm the identification of the dead man, other than that he had been 'deaf and dumb', and they were trying to trace relatives.

The confirmation that the dead man was Deaf caused some residents to mistakenly assume that he had been their neighbour from the 14th floor. One told reporters eager for news, "It's quite depressing. He was quite a friendly man. I had a drink with him in the Portobello just yesterday. It's quite a shock. I heard a bang outside in the early hours but we get a lot of kids round here and I thought it was a football or something. I found out what happened when the police came round this morning."

Police stated they were still pursuing door-to-door inquiries in the tower block, and had removed a number of items for forensic tests.

One item taken away by police from Peffermill Court included the tape from the building's security camera. Apart from capturing the horrific impact on the ground, the camera also showed just over two hours earlier two men at the lift, the smaller one gesticulating with his hands. The two men appeared to be arguing.

The next day, Meldrum Hazell, aged 33, unemployed of Flat 14/1 Peffermill Court appeared before Edinburgh Sheriff's Court charged with the murder of John Sutherland, aged 48, unemployed, of 12/2 Harewood Drive, Craigmillar, Edinburgh, and was remanded in custody to await trial. Both men were stated by the court to be 'deaf and dumb'.

Meldrum Hazell was born on 18th April 1961 in Glenrothes, Fife, the third of five children. At the age of four, he developed jaundice which left him almost totally deaf, and his mother helped him to develop his limited speech which saw his education through in a partially hearing unit. She died while Hazell was still quite young, and Hazell had a stormy relationship with his father as a result. It was that stormy relationship which led to his first serious offence, when Hazell assaulted his father, also named Meldrum, in a drunken rage after smashing down a door.

A persistent drink problem brought out an increasingly violent side to his personality, leading him to be charged with a string of public order offences, and a court order to attend a rehabilitation unit, which he attended for four years whilst making a fruitless search for permanent work. Following his time in the rehabilitation unit, Hazell moved into a specially-adapted flat on the top floor of Peffermill Court.

He became a regular, if occasionally unwelcome because of his habitual drunkenness, customer in public houses in his locality and he had been drinking since early afternoon on the day his violence took him past the point of no return.

The victim, John Sutherland, was as unfortunate a character as his killer. Born Deaf on 22nd December 1945 to an unmarried mother, he was a Christmas gift she had not wanted, and after a brief sight of the newly-born child, she handed him over to the Sisters of Charity for an orphan's upbringing and an education at the St.Vincent's School for Deaf Children in Glasgow. He was not only Deaf and unable to speak properly, he also had a harelip which made him more acutely aware of his difference from other children.

It was not until he was well into his 20's that John Sutherland first met his mother when he turned up out of the blue on the doorstep of her Edinburgh home. The meeting did not turn out well. His mother had never wanted anything to do with her bastard child, and although he discovered he had a sister, Irene, family relations in general were always strained due to Sutherland's liking for drink.

"When he stayed off the drink, he was quite a nice chap," said Paul MacDonald, his brother-in-law with whom the victim lived for about a year in 1991 in his sister's house, "But as the years went by, he got deeper into this belief that everyone was against him. He found it difficult to make friends, as his quick temper tended to put a lot of people off him."

During his stay with Irene and Paul MacDonald, his drinking and his temper got more and more oppressive leading to an incident when he fell out of an upper floor window in a drunken suicide threat, and broke an arm and a leg. Once he had recovered in hospital from these injuries, his sister and her husband asked him to leave and find other lodgings, which he did by finding a flat in Harewood Drive, Craigmillar.

Unemployed at the time of his death, Sutherland had many stretches out of work, but for a period of three years from 1989 to 1992, he had a steady job assembling scientific models at the University of Edinburgh, a job that gave him a lot of enjoyment and satisfaction.

When he lost that job following his suicide bid, Sutherland became very depressed and took to drink more and more.

One of the few friends that he had, a John Burns, a hearing man who had learnt sign language to communicate with his Deaf daughter, had this to say to reporters: "He was a good-hearted wee fella. If he had a shilling in his pocket, he'd give you half of it, that's the sort of guy he was. He was always buying people drinks, but he was always a very private person and deep down, he was lonely and used to get very depressed."

Although Sutherland would seem to disappear from the scene for long stretches of time, keeping to himself in his flat on Harewood Drive, he was a regular at the Castle Tavern on Niddrie Mains Road where other Deaf people would occasionally taunt or needle him for his scruffy clothes and unshaven appearance.

It was at the Castle Tavern on the evening of Wednesday 5th January that Sutherland ended up as a drinking companion of Meldrum Hazell, who also frequented the pub on occasion. They had met several times there in recent months, and on the last evening of his life, other Deaf pub customers remembered Hazell and Sutherland arguing about sexual conquests with one of the barmaids at the Castle Tavern. Both men made the unlikely claim to have bedded her. However, the argument died down, and later the two men left together. Originally, Sutherland had intended to go to Burns' house but instead had opted to make the fatal decision to accept the offer of a meal from Meldrum Hazell.

At his trial in Edinburgh High Court on 27th April 1994 before Lord Weir, Meldrum Hazell denied murdering John Sutherland, lodging through his counsel Neil Murray, Q.C., a special defence of self-defence.

Hazell followed the trial through sign language interpretation, and video screens displaying speech-to-text progress of the trial.

The court heard from pathologist Dr. Basil Purdoe that it had been difficult to track some of the 18 stab wounds found on the body because the internal organs had been so 'scrambled' and many of the main bones fragmented in the plunge from the 14th floor of Peffermill Court. The pathologist gave it as his opinion that Sutherland had either been dead or dying before he hit the ground.

Detective Constable Michael Watt told the court that they had found 'footprints in blood' inside Hazell's flat, and that he had been found sitting dazed on a couch. Watt said that Hazell's mood had swung from relaxed and jovial to reflective and depressed during the police interview as he tried to explain how he had shoved the body out of his window because he could not stand the sight of the blood.

"John's back was wide open and so was his front. That is why I put him out of the window. My hand went into the wound. I had to wash it off. I felt sick and I was sick. I never murdered before. I don't know why I did it," Hazell was alleged to have told Watt, who was reading from his notes.

Speaking in his own defence, Hazell told defence counsel Neil Murray through sign language interpreters that he had met up with Sutherland in the Castle Tavern public house the evening of 5th January, and had invited Sutherland back to his flat after the victim had told him he had no food in his own house and was hungry.

After the meal, Hazell said that he had gone to bed after Sutherland had said he did not want to go to his own flat about half-a-mile away. He had given Sutherland a blanket and pillows, and had left him watching a video called 'Children of a Lesser God', a film about a romance between a Deaf girl and a teacher set in America which Sutherland said he had never seen. Hazell said that he thought Sutherland had more to drink than was good for him, which was why he felt disinclined to go to his own home.

Hazell alleged that in the middle of the night, he was woken up by Sutherland switching the lights on in his bedroom. Sutherland was carrying a knife and was dressed only in his underpants, and came and lay down on the top of Hazell's duvet, and tried to strike him with the knife.

Asked by defence counsel Murray what he thought Sutherland was doing coming into his bedroom with a knife, Hazell replied : "I thought he was making a homosexual advance."

Hazell said that in self-defence, he had pushed the knife away, and it had gone into Sutherland. A struggle then began and lasted about five or ten minutes when he managed to disarm Sutherland and stab him a number of times.

He remembered seeing blood on the walls, and Sutherland lying still, and said that he had panicked because he could not stand the sight of blood, and did not know what to do with the body. That was then that Hazell decided to throw his victim out of the window.

Jailing Hazell after a guilty verdict was brought in by the jury, Lord Weir said that there was only one sentence he could give, and sentenced him to life imprisonment.

As Meldrum Hazell was led away to begin his life sentence, people sought to seek a motive for the meaningless crime. Hazell had repeatedly replied to such questions, "I don't know."

He is now behind bars, but the mystery still remains.

19 :   1994 London

THE PORNO CINEMA FIRE

From the outside, number seven St. John Street looked like a rather dilapidated office block.   The ground floor housed the City Coffee House, a grand name for a poorly furnished and run-down cafe.   The area was situated very near to London's famous Smithfield Market.

But to the people in suits and others who went inside, furtively reaching in their pockets for the £7 entry fee, the building housed on its upper floors a private cinema known variously as the New City Cinema Club, or the Dream City Club.   Unlike the nearby red-light district of Soho where private cinema clubs flourish alongside peep shows, strip joints and sex shops, the New City Cinema Club displayed no neon lights advertising its presence, and there was not even a discreet nameplate on the front door.

The four storey building housed makeshift cinemas on its first and second floors each able to sit up to 30 customers, whilst the top floor contained a video storeroom, and another empty room which had previously been a massage parlour. Taking advantage of a loophole in the strict licensing laws designed to aid fire prevention by calling itself a private club rather than as a public cinema, the New City did not have a cinema licence, and had twice - in 1988 and 1990 - been prosecuted by the local council, Islington, for running an unlicensed cinema. Fines totalled more than £1000 and equipment was also seized.   Even then, Islington Council was unsuccessful in tracing the true owners of the club and had to take its lowly managers to court, and had been unable to gain entry to undertake a fire, health and safety inspection.

Meldrum Hazell being led away to a life sentence. (Chapter 18)

A body being removed from The Cinema Club. (Chapter 19)

Fire officers investigating the arson-murder scene. (Chapter 19)

Tracy Turner. (Chapter 20)

Looking down Malmesbury Road towards the victim's house. (Chapter 21)

Track of bloody footprints. (Chapter 21)

Still, the New City continued to operate, acting as a mecca for men such as respected businessmen who would go secure in the knowledge they would not be recognised, for sexual stimulation, the secrecy element of sneaking into a porno cinema adding to their excitement of a "naughty but nice" activity of watching blue films containing loads of young girls. Other customers would be lonely men without partners, or married men only able to ease their sexual frustration by watching gay movies. Some gay men would also see such cinemas like New City as ideal venues for picking up other men for anonymous sex, particularly on nights when gay films were scheduled to be shown.

On Saturday 26th February 1994, both cinemas were in use on the first and second floors showing pornographic heterosexual films when, at approximately 5 p.m., there was an argument outside the doorway of the New City club between the doorman, Anthony Parsons, and a slightly stooped man of approximately 35 years of age wearing a dark jacket who was being refused entry because he seemed to be drunk. A punch was thrown before the man was headbutted by Parsons, and ejected from the building.

A little later, just after 5.38 p.m., a man carrying a red fuel can was seen running away in the direction of nearby Farringdon underground train station just as flames were spotted coming out of the doorway of the dingy entrance to the New City club.

By the time the first fire engines and ambulances had arrived on the scene at 5.46 p.m., the building was a roaring inferno. The choking screams of men gasping for air in the acrid smoke echoed around the area as they panicked and stumbled around blindly looking for escape, but passers-by and rescuers could only look on helplessly, driven back by the searing heat, as the inferno engulfed the stairway.

"They were weird, blood-curling screams of very frightened people," said one.

Desperate cinema customers started kicking out the first and second floor windows, and began to hurl themselves into St. John Street. The thuds as they landed, and bones being broken, could be heard by those outside.

Workers from Pickfords, a furniture removals company, who had been shifting furniture from an office block a few doors away, placed their tall furniture van directly underneath some of the windows and encouraged some people to jump onto it before they were told to move it away by fire officers on the scene because of the danger of diesel fuel exploding and adding to the inferno.

Many of those who escaped did so by way of jumping onto, and clambering down fire-fighters' platform ladders in their panic, disregarding the danger of knocking off fire-fighters who were trying to *climb up* the ladders.

Eventually, firemen managed to restore some form of control, and started to bring out dead and badly injured bodies, which had smoke still coming off them as they were being brought out. One badly injured man was rescued off the roof of the furniture van onto which he had jumped, but was in no state to move any further.

The injured were rushed to nearby St. Barts and University College hospitals, and also to the Royal London in Whitechapel, where - still trying to preserve their anonymity to the end - some gave false names such as John Smith or James Brown.

As police and fire investigators began to search the smoking ruins for evidence as to the cause of the blaze late that night, police announced that eight people, all men, were dead and 20 others were seriously injured in a number of hospitals, at least six of them in intensive care including one man who had suffered multiple injuries from jumping from a second floor window.

The search for evidence also found that the New City Cinema Club had become a death-trap for those who had paid for a few hours pleasure. The only exit was the rickety stairway onto which had been poured a large capacity of inflammable fluid engulfing it immediately in flames, trapping all the victims above. Although the club had been granted a fire brigade certificate in 1990, there were no fire escape ladders at the back of the building, no sprinklers inside the club premises and preciously few extinguishers. A door which led to a third floor rear exit was nailed shut to discourage gatecrashers and sexual activity, and a window which could have provided an escape route was covered up by a false wall. There had been desperate attempts to smash it down.

The running man with the red petrol can seen minutes before the inferno was soon brought to the attention of investigators, and immediately became the prime suspect. Enquiries in the area soon elicited the fact the same man, or someone very much like him, had bought from a Texaco service station on Clerkenwell Road a short 400 yards walk away from St. John Street a red container of petrol, tendering a £10 note in payment. The cashier, Ponniah Ganeshamoorthy, told police officers that it had been the only can he had sold all that day.

The man had not said a word during the purchase of the petrol can, and had left on foot in a hurry. As police officers continued to carry out inquiries, Detective Superintendent John Chaplin, leading the hunt for the arsonist, gave out a detailed description of a man the police were particularly anxious to interview and eliminate from their inquiries.

On Monday evening, a man walked into Walthamstow police station in east London and admitted responsibility for the torching of the New City club. He was arrested, and transferred to Islington police station for further questioning, which could not be proceeded with until the services of a sign language interpreter were obtained.

On Thursday 3rd March 1994, a man appeared before Highbury Corner Magistrates Court accused of killing nine men - one of the critically injured had died in hospital since the fire. He followed proceedings through a sign language interpreter and was remanded in custody pending further enquiries. He was named as David Lauwers, aged 34 of no fixed address but living in Walthamstow, where he worked in a clothing factory as a pattern cutter.

David Lauwers originally came to London from Scotland as a teenager in 1980. In London, he had lived alone in a series of bedsits, eking out a living with a low-paid job as a cutter and presser with Springtime Fashions in Walthamstow for 15 years. Lauwers rarely mixed with other Deaf people, and was almost unknown in the capital's Deaf Community. Those who did know him, or of him, knew him as an alcoholic. One deaf landlady, a Patricia Hill who once rented him a flat, said of him, "He got drunk every day. He was a very lonely man, and the only friends he had were drinking friends."

He was sometimes seen frequenting public houses and other venues where gay men socialised but also kept to himself a great deal of the time. He was known to a few Deaf gay men in the London scene, but often shied away from conversation or socialising with them. They believed he was a closet homosexual, sexually frustrated but unable to come to terms with himself. He was unmarried, and only once had he had a girlfriend, and that had been some years back.

He had been a member of New City Cinema Club for some years, and was a regular customer there where he was known for his liking for drink, and had previously been ejected from the private cinema for drunkenness, and was regarded as a bit of a nuisance. He was particularly keen on watching hard-core pornographic films, but was not known to have had any sexual liaisons there or been picked up by anyone.

Police also discovered that Lauwers had a record as a minor criminal, with strings of convictions for theft, assault and criminal damage. Sentences had included probation, a conditional discharge and fines.

On the night of Wednesday 16th March 1994, more than two weeks after the fire, a man named James Miller, aged 49, died in hospital where he had been in a critical condition since being admitted, bringing the total number of deaths occurring as a result of the fire to eleven, one other person also having died about a week after the fire.

At the Old Bailey on 21st March 1995, David Lauwers appeared before Sir Lawrence Verney, the Recorder for London, accused of three representative charges of murder and one of murder with intent to endanger life. He pleaded not guilty through a sign language interpreter.

The court was told that on 26th February the previous year, the accused had appeared drunk before the cash office where Anthony Parsons was sitting with another man named James Miller and had tried to tell them in his poor speech he had already been watching porn movies at the cinema earlier that day, and refused to pay the £7 entrance fee. Parsons refused to accept that Lauwers had been there earlier in the day or that he was a member of the club, as Lauwers was unable to furnish proof of his membership card, and demanded that Lauwers pay both the entrance fee and the annual membership fee of £5. Lauwers had become increasingly argumentative and aggressive when asked to leave and had thrown a punch at Parsons who then headbutted the accused and ejected him from the premises.

The court then heard from John Nutting, prosecuting counsel, that Lauwers had walked to a nearby Texaco petrol station and purchased a can of petrol, and gone back to the New City cinema where he then firebombed the stairway.

Mr.Nutting said that the cinema was rapidly engulfed in flames and choking smoke as Lauwers made his escape. "The fire took hold at great speed, shutting off any means of escape through the ground floor entrance lobby. The electric lights went out and dense smoke quickly rose up through the building. There were about 30 men in the two cinemas. Pandemonium broke out as they realised the mortal danger they faced. Some tried to descend the main staircase, but were driven back by the intensity of the heat, and were unable to breathe."

The prosecuting counsel went on to state that some were killed as they jumped from the four-storey building. Others were trapped by locked doors and barred windows, lost consciousness and died in the thick smoke. As well as the eleven men who died, fifteen men were seriously injured. Lauwers, he said, had been seen running to Farringdon Road underground station.

Rock Tansey, QC, representing Lauwers said that his client had never intended to cause anyone serious injury. Lauwers had returned from Farringdon Road to a bedsit in Higham Road, Walthamstow where he was staying with a friend, calling at an off-licence on the way to buy six cans of lager, and had been stupefied and terrified when the television news brought home to him what he had done.

Some of the witnesses called before the court had their anonymity preserved under a court order. A witness named only as Mr.Y said he had seen Lauwers acting strangely outside the club shortly before the blaze, and said he had tried to get down the stairs but could not make it to the first floor because of the black smoke, and had jumped to safety from a second floor window. Another witness, Mr.Z, stated that he could not get out and had found a fire escape door nailed shut. He had laid down, and lost consciousness.

A witness named as Mr.X described the horrific scenes in the second floor cinema as he clambered onto a window ledge. Several men about to die were wailing for their families, while others knelt and recited the Lord's Prayer. "The worse aspect," he said, "was that it wasn't screaming from people who were burning alive. It was primal, more a primal howl of people in deep pain burning to death. There was also the stench of burning flesh."

Mr.X, who said he was in his late 30's, had been several times to the private, members-only cinema and knew there was a window on the second floor not boarded up, and had headed for it, and smashed it with a chair, and jumped out onto the ledge. Thick black smoke was pouring out behind him. There was nothing to drop on to, and he held himself on the ledge by digging his hand into the broken glass in the window frame. He tried to find another way down, but the smoke in the room was too thick to allow him to breathe and he returned to the ledge where desperate men were pushing past him as they scrambled to get out. Fire engines had arrived but were still trying to extend their ladders.

"I looked up to the sky, partly to be able to breathe, partly just really to speak to my deceased parents who were always very good to me and said to them, 'please help me to make the right choice'. I told the emergency services I could not hold on any longer and that I was going to jump. They were shouting to hang on, but it just wasn't possible. I was on fire."

Mr.X broke his left foot and ankle, left knee and pelvis in eight places, his left elbow, wrist and a rib when he jumped, and also suffered a spinal injury, and was in hospital for almost two months. Nine pins were holding his rebuilt pelvis together.

Two employees of Pickfords Removals whose van was placed under a first floor window to provide an escape route also gave evidence. One, Liam Thornton, told the court :"I would say that within about three to five minutes of the first flames, the whole building was a furnace."

Richard Chambers, another Pickfords worker, stated: "One minute it appeared to be OK, the next there was a type of big whoosh and there were smoke and flames everywhere. It all happened in an instant. There were lots of men at the windows. You could see the wall of flames behind them. I remember seeing one guy come out of the window in a diving position. He went through the air and his head was turning under him. He hit the ground with a hell of a thud and from the noise, I assumed he hit the ground with his head."

Anthony Parsons, who was one of those who escaped the fire by jumping onto the Pickfords Removals van, gave evidence of the altercation with Lauwers which resulted in his ejection from the club and directly led to the act of revenge where the accused firebombed the premises. He stated that he had acted in self defence because Lauwers had become so aggressive. This evidence could not be collaborated as James Miller, who had been in the cash office with him at the time of the fracas, had died in hospital of his injuries over two weeks after the fire.

A sub officer with the London Fire Brigade, Peter Banks, agreed with the defence counsel, Rock Tansey, that inside the cinema there were three possible exits apart from the stairway which had been blocked. One door had been nailed shut, another sealed up and a third was padlocked, and this had contributed significantly to the high death toll.

On the fourth day of the trial, a statement from a John Carson was read before the court. The witness was too ill with cancer to attend the Old Bailey.

In his statement, the witness stated that he had seen Lauwers start the fire, and had followed him at a fast jog to Farringdon Road underground station a few hundred yards away where Lauwers had twice switched platforms before making off on a westbound train. Carson attested that he had only discovered how serious the fire was when he went back to St.John Street. He was able to identify Lauwers in an identity parade after the accused had given himself up.

Mr.Tansey, defence counsel, requested that he make a presentation to the court in absence of the jury, and the Recorder then asked for the jury to leave the room. Mr.Tansey admitted in the jury's absence that John Carson's statement had sealed his client's fate, and David Lauwers now wished to plead guilty to manslaughter. The prosecution, however, stated they wished to pursue the trial to press for a murder conviction.

On 27th March, the jury retired to consider their verdicts and found David Lauwers not guilty of the three representative charges of murder. However, they found the accused guilty of eleven counts of manslaughter, and one of reckless arson.

There were cries of "bastard!" in the public gallery as Lauwers past record was revealed. This included the fact that he had a previous conviction for arson. This related to his only relationship with a girl in the early 1980's when she told him their relationship was over. His response had chilling parallels to the New City Cinema club fire. As with the cinema club fire, he had gone to a garage and filled a petrol can, and returned to her flat and firebombed it. Fortunately at that time, there was no-one in it. He had then gone to the pub where she was drinking with friends and told her that her home was on fire, then sat down calmly drinking until the police arrived to arrest him.

At the trial for this arson at the Old Bailey, the sitting judge, Mr. Justice Alliott, was swayed by a string of glowing testimonials given on behalf of Lauwers, with the end result that he was only given two year's probation for this crime. It was said that this lenient sentence may have given Lauwers the impression that he could get away with it easily again.

Sir Lawrence Verney, in sentencing Lauwers, said he agreed with the jury's verdict, and that because the outcome of Lauwer's simple act of revenge had been so horrific, the only sentence he could give was a life sentence, with a recommendation that a minimum of ten years be served.

This brought forth further protests from relatives of those who had perished in the fire, claiming it was too lenient. One stormed : "It means less than a year for every life he claimed."

The total of eleven deaths in this case is the highest number of murders by a Deaf person.

20 : 1994 Leicestershire

THE LAST RIDE

The man walking his dog in the early hours of Friday 4th March 1994 spotted the body, after investigating what his dog was getting all excited about.

The woman's body was naked and lay on its back on the grass verge of the quiet country lane with its head towards the hedgerow. Short and stocky, with dirty blonde hair, she was obviously dead, and the man placed the call to Leicestershire Constabulary which was to see them struggle for nearly two weeks to identify the corpse.

The quiet lane known as Woodby Lane, in fields near Bitteswell, a small village near Lutterworth in Leicestershire, was popular with courting couples and local people walking their dogs. No attempt had been made to hide the body, and if the person who had dumped it there thought it would be sometime before it was found, he or she was badly mistaken because although quiet, Woodby Lane was well-used. and the body was bound to be discovered sooner rather than later.

A police squad led by Detective Sergeant Dave Marshall arrived in response to the dog-walker's call, and soon sealed off the lane to preserve the crime scene, and set up a murder inquiry incident room in a mobile van. Later, Detective Superintendent Ian Stripp of Leicestershire C.I.D. arrived to take charge of the murder investigation.

It was soon established that the woman had been strangled, and that she had been engaged in enthusiastic sex just prior to her death. In the words of one police officer, 'she had been well and truly shafted.'

From the start of the investigation, police were seriously hampered by not knowing the identity of the dead woman.

The victim was described as aged approximately 25 to 35, 5 foot 1 inch tall, and weighed thirteen stone. She was quite busty, with a bust size of 46 inches, and was also big in the hips. She had natural light blonde hair which had not been cut for some time, and a body which showed that she did not look after herself well. For example, all her fingernails were bitten right down, and her toenails were unkempt.

It was estimated that she had been killed anytime up to 12 hours before the body had been discovered.

It did not help that at the same time, all national newspapers were focused on what was happening at 25 Cromwell Street, Gloucester, reporting every macabre dig being conducted by police investigators there, and every body that was recovered from the house occupied by Fred and Rosemary West. The finding of a single dead female body in rural Leicestershire paled into insignificance with one of the most sensational murder investigations of the century, and little publicity was therefore given by the national press to the Leicestershire murder.

Police appealed for members of the public and any witnesses who might have been in the vicinity of Woodby Lane on the night of 3rd/4th March to come forward and assist the police in their enquiries and elimination.

Residents of the nearby village of Bitteswell expressed shock at the murder, but the woman was a stranger to the village, and none could help. Two witnesses who had been driving past in a car at 6.50 a.m. the morning of 4th March spoke of seeing a grey-haired man of approximately 40-50 years of age standing on a grass verge beside Bitteswell Football Club ground near Woodby Lane looking agitated, and the landlord of the local inn spoke of a woman of similar description to the victim who had never been to his place before eating a meal with some gusto in the company of a man. None of these leads produced anything.

In their efforts to trace the victim, over 20 police officers conducted a fingertip search of Woodby Lane, and examined tyre prints without any success.

"The woman was too heavy to be carried easily," said one police source, "so someone would have to stop their vehicle and drag her out before dumping her."

To the police, this seemed a most likely explanation of how the dead woman had got to the lane as no trace of the woman's clothes was found at the murder scene, nor anything which might be linked with the woman. If this had happened, a lorry or a van would have had to reverse back down the lane, but a car could have just turned around.

To police officers, there were some similarities to the murder of a Birmingham prostitute, Samo Paull, whose body had been found in a water-filled ditch on 30th December 1993, just over two months earlier, at Swinford, a bare 2 miles away, and detectives liaised with the West Midlands police to investigate the possibility the two murders were linked.

As the days went by, and police got no further clues, they turned to other measures. These included calling in a leading British psychologist, Paul Britton, who was based at Leicester's Towers Hospital, to draw up a profile of the killer. Mr.Britton had helped police previously with accurate profiles of the kidnapper Michael Sams and of the two boys who had killed Jamie Bulger in Liverpool.

Another avenue they tried was to call in cosmetics and hairdressing experts who advised a local trainee funeral director, Shaun Gosling, to make up the victim's face to make it look lifelike. The result was photographed and circulated to the press.

They also circulated details of the victim's teeth to over 16,000 dental practices throughout the country.

One week after the murder, with still no leads, and with national newspapers still focused on the West murders in Gloucestershire - for example, on 8th March, newspapers carried the news that the seventh body had been recovered from the 'house of horrors', as the Wests' home was being called - Leicestershire police took the unusual step of paying for an advertisement to be placed in one of the national daily newspapers, The Sun.

The morning television channel, GMTV, also featured the appeal by the Leicestershire police.

At last, two leads came up which were to lead police to identify the dead woman.

One lead came from a man living in London to say he owned properties which he rented out in Stafford, and he thought that the woman looked like one of his tenants, whom he had only met twice.

The other lead came from a Stafford newspaper reporter, a Sally Blower, who told police she thought the victim looked like her next door neighbour, whom she had not seen for at least two weeks.

Following these two tip-offs police went to the identified flat in Stafford, and sealed off the property which was subjected to an exhaustive search.

On 17th March, thirteen days after the murder, police were finally to announce that they had identified the victim as a Tracy Lynn Turner, aged 30. Her father, William Turner, who lived apart from her mother, was traced to an address in Rotherham, South Yorkshire, and brought down to identify the body.

With a name to go on, police were now to make some progress and draw up a profile on Tracy Turner and her lifestyle, which they found to be slightly unusual.

They found that she was profoundly deaf, with a 75% loss in one ear, and 50% loss in the other, and always wore a hearing aid of the cord-type. She had gone to a unit for hearing-impaired children in Sheffield, and had left home at the age of 15, travelling the country. At one stage, she worked as a prostitute in the Kings Cross area of London before returning north and taking up a flat in Stafford about a year before her death.

Tracy Turner was unemployed, but had a 'buzz' and an affinity for truckers. She loved to travel around the country in lorries. Her 'fare' was usually sex, selling herself for pin money and get lifts so that she could look at the passing countryside from lorry cabs.

She was described by her next-door neighbour Sally Blower as a strange character who liked to rummage in trash bins, and who had once set fire to Ms.Blower's bin. She was frequently unkempt and dirty, a loner who found it difficult to mix with other people.

In fact, she fell into that category of people known to the Deaf Community as someone who 'fitted neither in the Deaf world or the hearing world' because of their type of education and their deafness.

It was not just the fact she was deaf which caused her to be a loner. It was also her size. She was a very noticeable girl whose mass of light blonde hair and size made her look a very big, powerful girl.

Police found that she was recognised by prostitutes in the Kings Cross area of London, and also the red-light area of Balsall Heath in Birmingham (where incidentally Samo Paull also worked her trade). She was also recognised by people frequenting or working in service stations on the M1 and M6 as a regular 'trunk groupie' although most of them did not know her name.

Police found that on her last day, she had withdrawn £5 from a building society account in Stafford, and that by 10.40 p.m. on the night of 3 March, she had arrived at Hilton Park (Birmingham North) service station on the M6, which was a few miles down the motorway from Stafford.

She was last seen at 12.40 a.m. on the southern slip road to the M6 heading for London, and a reliable witness insisted she was not there 20 minutes later at 1 a.m.

She was last seen wearing a dark green anorak, black or dark grey leggings, and was carrying a holdall which she always carried, which contained spare clothing and toiletries.

Seven hours later, she was found 40 miles away, and depending on the type of vehicle, the journey would have taken roughly three-quarters of an hour. Bitteswell itself is a very rural village but very close to both M1, M6 and M69 motorways, and also the A5 and A14 main trunk roads, the sort of roads lorries would frequent.

No trace of her clothing or her holdall has ever been found, nor her hearing aid which she always wore. It was not in her flat at Stafford either, and it was believed by police that all her property had been deliberately destroyed or hidden to prevent any link to the murderer.

In fact, the post-mortem revealed that Tracy was strangled with a very thin piece of cable, and police believe that it may even have been her hearing-aid cord that was used to strangle her as there were no finger-marks on her, and she had been attacked from behind. There were faint bruises near the small of her back which could have been caused by a knee or a foot holding her from behind whilst the cable or cord was used to strangle her. Scratch marks on her cheeks and neck were made by Tracy herself, probably as she tried to remove or free herself from whatever was around her neck.

Police believe that if she had been attacked from the front, she would have fought for herself, and being a strong girl, would have had defence marks, and they believe she was killed elsewhere and her body dumped in Woodby Lane.

Despite widespread inquiries, police have never found a lorry-driver who had admitted giving her a lift.

"It is often against transport company rules to give lifts," said a police source, "but we know she travelled all over Britain, maybe even Ireland and Europe, in lorries, and if anyone came forward to give us any information about Tracy and her lifts, we would deal with it in total confidence."

Police have not entirely discounted any connection with the killing of Samo Paull, despite having no evidence to link the two cases, but are inclined to think that it is pure coincidence that the bodies of two women who sold their bodies for sex were dumped so close together.

"I have no doubt the murderer will be caught eventually," Detective Superintendent Stripp is reported to have said, "I also believe that somebody out there knows something they are not telling us, maybe out of fear, maybe out of loyalty."

If the police have any DNA evidence, taken from Tracy's last enthusiastic sexual adventure that led to her death, they are not telling, but at the time of writing this book (October 1997), the case is still unsolved but not forgotten by police.

Tracy Turner was a sad, lonely deaf girl who met a horrible end through her 'hobby' of sex and riding in lorries, and we can only hope that the murderer will be caught one day.

21 :   1994 Wimbledon, London

THE MILLION POUND MISTAKE

The summer of 1995 was not a good one for the British judiciary which did not seem to have learnt from past mistakes, and from meetings held between the Lord Chancellor's Office and senior officials of the main charities for Deaf people, the British Deaf Association and the Royal National Institute for Deaf people, aimed at ensuring that representation of Deaf people appearing before criminal courts was fair and clarifying issues around sign language interpretation of criminal trials.

This did not prevent one learned Judge presiding over a trial at the Old Bailey from issuing threats against a Deaf organisation.

What happened was that a court case involving a Deaf defendant accused of rape had to be postponed on 11th September because only one fully qualified sign language interpreter was present instead of the normal two interpreters which should be provided to allow for suitable breaks necessary for avoiding mistakes caused by tiredness, and also to check for accuracy. Mr.Justice Bruce Laughland refused to accept that one interpreter could not do the job and tried to get the trial started by overruling the need for a second interpreter, but the original interpreter decided to withdraw his services to avoid compromising the defendant's right to a fair trial.

During an exchange with the judge, the interpreter said: "I think I would be very severely criticised by my profession if I agreed to go ahead this morning."

"Could you not say to them," said the judge, 'I am afraid that a very disagreeable, overbearing judge who did not really understand, he made me'."

"I think I would be open," responded the interpreter, "to having my name crossed off the register of sign language interpreters if I went ahead this morning."

"Well, I hope not!", the judge said, "I take a very serious view. I think that it would be contempt of court if that happened and I would take a very serious view of anyone who took that step, if you had complied with my earnest request to assist the administration of justice, as I do, and anyone who struck your name off the list would be here at once for it and they might go inside for three months."

This did not sway the interpreter. Earlier in the exchange, the interpreter had stated that to go ahead with the trial would not be 'in the interests of justice', to which the judge had retorted, "I am the guardian of what is just."

Faced with having to postpone the trial, Judge Laughland erupted and lambasted the British Deaf Association, threatening to "write to the Secretary of State for Health" to oppose the BDA receiving any public money.

The BDA hit back through an official spokesperson :"It is outrageous that a judge should make these threats in an attempt to undermine the BDA's position. Having accurate access to court proceedings and obtaining a fair trial is of huge importance for Deaf people. This attitude shows an immediate need for the Judge to undertake a Deaf Awareness course if he is to act fairly in judging a case involving a Deaf person. The BDA fully supports the position that there should be two qualified independent interpreters in such a trial. No responsible interpreter would single-handedly take on such an assignment. We call upon the Lord Chancellor's Office to issue guidelines to courts in making clear the vital need to have this level of interpretation if Deaf people are to receive fair trials."

The Royal National Institute for Deaf people, though not named by Judge Laughland, were equally uncompromising in supporting the BDA's stance: "It is intolerable that this case was postponed solely because the defendant was deaf and the court had not provided suitable communication support. The interpreter was entitled to ask for assistance as interpreting is tiring and mistakes can be made due to fatigue. Mistakes in a trial could be detrimental to the course of justice and possibly prevent a fair outcome."

To reinforce these firm stances, in the same week a court case collapsed in a different court which clearly highlighted the need for accuracy in sign language interpretation. This one was in Reading Crown Court where a Deaf person also stood accused of rape.

On this occasion, the qualified court Sign Language interpreters noticed that the statement made by the accused during the police interviews after he had been arrested did not match what he was saying in court, and it was discovered that the interpreter who had been present at the man's interview in the police station had not properly understood or translated what the Deaf man had been saying. The presiding judge felt there was no alternative but to send the jury home, and postpone the trial.

In a follow up to comments made after Judge Laughland's outburst, the BDA said : "This adds strength to the BDA's argument for emergency funding to increase the number of qualified interpreters. The Government has failed, and until it does, the possibility of this kind of problem happening again is very real."

The uncompromising stance of the BDA and the RNID arose from another court case at the Old Bailey earlier that summer where two Deaf defendants stood along with a hearing individual all accused of murder, and the trial had already been in progress for eight weeks when the sign language interpreter made an error during the defence stage which was caused, he said, through tiredness.

In the absence of the jury, defence lawyers argued the point that the misinterpretation could influence the jury's view even if a new interpreter was used and the jurors were instructed to disregard what they had heard earlier.

Presiding Judge Nina Lowry ordered a new trial, stating : "The position is that I cannot continue the trial without there being a danger to one or other of these defendants and there is no point in continuing if there is a danger of justice."

Despite the blunder, Judge Lowry praised all the interpreters involved. "Every interpreter in this case has striven to fulfil a difficult task with skill and integrity. There is a small crumb of comfort that this unusual, if not unique, case where so many of the witnesses and defendants were deaf had provided invaluable lessons learnt for the future."

It evidently did not for Judge Laughland a bare three months later!

The trial that had been before Judge Nina Lowry had already cost a million pounds when it was halted, and had its beginnings one warm August night a year earlier.

On the morning of Wednesday 3 August 1994, a concerned neighbour noticed that the ground floor kitchen window of pensioner Frederick Clancey's house at 108 Malmesbury Road, Morden in South London was broken, and that there was blood on the window sill.

The neighbour was aware that frail 65 year-old Fred Clancey had been a victim of several break-ins in recent weeks, and decided to call the police.

The neighbour's call was logged at Wimbledon police station, which sent a panda car to investigate. The first officers to arrive on the scene were to report back to Wimbledon police station confirming that there were indications that a burglary had taken place at the house in Malmesbury Road, but they were unable to elicit any response from the occupant, and were going to effect entry to investigate further.

The officers were horrified to discover the battered and bloodied body of the old man lying in the kitchen of his house, and put through a call for a Scene of Crimes unit to be dispatched to the house.

To investigating officers, it was obvious that Clancey had disturbed a burglary in progress, entry having been effected through the smashed window, and had fought for his life in the kitchen which showed signs that a considerable struggle had taken place in that room. Blood was splattered over the walls, and a pool of blood spilled around where the body lay. Footprints in blood from different size shoes were on the floor in places, showing that there had been more than one assailant doing the burglary that had disturbed the elderly pensioner.

To the investigating detectives, the bloody footprints were a godsend. Clearly, the murderers had not realised in the dark of the night they were laying out a trail, and that trail led detectives straight to a neighbouring house at 145 Malmesbury Road where lived a young woman in her twenties and her current juvenile boyfriend, who were both promptly arrested and taken to Wimbledon police station for questioning. A warrant was also applied for from magistrates to search the house where the pair were arrested.

Meanwhile, a post mortem was carried out on Frederick Clancey, and this found that besides having a number of stab wounds, the victim had been severely beaten, stamped and kicked about the head and the neck.

Forensic experts and scene of crime officers spent the rest of the day gathering evidence from the two houses. From the murdered man's house, blood samples taken from a smashed cup - later in court stated to have been used by the pensioner as a weapon to try to defend himself by hitting one of the assailants on the head - were found to be a perfect match with the blood grouping of the 17 year-old juvenile.

From the smashed window, further blood samples were taken which proved to belong to the young woman, who had badly injured herself when breaking into her neighbour's house. The hand injury where she had cut herself was still evident at the time of her arrest.

From the pair's house along the road from the victim, blood-stained clothing belonging to the woman was recovered from the attic. Also recovered were articles and items found to have come from the murdered man's house, plus proceeds of other robberies.

Diligent questioning carried out back at the police station in Wimbledon, with the aid of a sign language interpreter, led police across south London later that day into the eastern part of the city, where they raided a house at Culverley Road, Catford and took into custody a 28 year-old man.

The following day, a 26 year-old Deaf woman, Joanne Lee Smith of Malmesbury Road, Morden, and her brother-in-law, Barry John Smith, of Culverley Road, Catford appeared briefly before Wimbledon Magistrates charged with the murder of Frederick Clancey and were remanded in custody for a week pending further police enquiries.

Later that week, an un-named juvenile aged 17, came up before the Juvenile Court, and was also remanded in custody, also charged with the murder.

Joanne Lee Smith was an ex-pupil of Oak Lodge School for Deaf Children in Wandsworth, and was separated from her husband. She had a reputation for violence, for which she had previous convictions and also for larceny and burglary. Barry Smith was also an ex-pupil of Oak Lodge School, and known to the police for petty misdemeanours. The juvenile, later named as Darren Sams, a hearing person, had a long record as a young offender.

On Tuesday 29th November, magistrates at Wimbledon committed all three accused persons to trial at the Old Bailey for murder. It was this trial before Judge Nina Lowry which collapsed after eight weeks at a cost of a million pounds during the defence stage after many witnesses, including Deaf witnesses, had given evidence. Sign Language interpretation had been given throughout the trial.

The re-trial commenced in September 1995 before Judge Gerald Gordon who had ordered this time that there should be adequate provision of qualified Sign Language interpreters available for the trial (one of the consequences of which meant that in another court of the Old Bailey at the same time, Judge Laughland was forced to postpone the trial before his court due to inadequate Sign Language interpretation being available to him.)

All three defendants pleaded not guilty to the charges of murder, and during the four week trial that followed, the jury heard the victim, Fred Clancey, being described as a mild and inoffensive old man who was plagued by repeated break-ins at his home in Morden.

The prosecution alleged that Joanne Smith and Darren Sams, who lived in the same road as Clancey, had been behind some of these robberies, regarding Clancey as an easy source of ready cash. A few days before the murder, the pair had been seen in deaf circles and in local pubs waving money around, boasting that it had come from Mr.Clancey.

On the evening of 2 August, the prosecution alleged that Joanne Smith and Sams were in a local pub where they were joined by Barry Smith, Joanne's brother-in-law, and fuelled by drink and running out of money, the three of them decided to repeat their robberies of Fred Clancey to get some more money, and at around midnight, Joanne Smith led them round to their potential victim's house, and broke through the kitchen window.

However, Joanne Smith had cut herself badly on the window, and the prosecution would show, through forensic witnesses, that the blood found at this particular scene matched that of Joanne Smith "without a single doubt."

The noise of the break-in had disturbed Mr.Clancey, and he had gone to investigate "armed only with a cup from which he had been drinking a late tea". The victim had hit Darren Sams over the head with this cup, breaking it.

Darren Sams, it was alleged, had gone to the scene of the crime armed with a crowbar and, enraged by having had a cup of tea smashed over his head, Sams used the crowbar to batter the old man down to the floor, where he was kicked, stamped and finally also stabbed. The post mortem findings would show that Fred Clancey had been stabbed fifteen times, and that he had also multiple injuries to the head, face and chest, some of which had show heelmarks to indicate that the assailants had stamped the victim ferociously.

If this was not enough, the assailants then pelted their victim with food as he lay on the floor defenceless.

All this, the prosecution said, had been done just for the sake of a few pounds.

In defence of Barry Smith, his counsel said that his client had not gone to Mr.Clancey's house with the intention of harming anyone. He had been told by his sister-in-law of some easy pickings, and had wanted some for himself. He had not taken part in much of the violence that followed Mr.Clancey disturbing the burglary in progress.

The jury heard that there had been so much blood spilled at the scene of the murder that it had been so easy for the police to follow a trail that led directly to the nearby house occupied by Joanne Smith and Sams, where they were then arrested and taken into custody. Blood-stained clothing and one of the murder weapons were also recovered by police from the house.

The jury returned verdicts of "Guilty" of murder against Joanne Smith and Darren Sams. Barry Smith was found not guilty of murder, but guilty of manslaughter.

In sentencing the three accused in the dock, Judge Gerald Gordon said: "No one who has listened to the evidence and seen the photographs could be other than revolted by the brutal and sustained attack which led to the death of a mild and inoffensive elderly man." The disturbance of the burglary by the victim did not, he said, justify the intensity and severity of the violence which had followed the discovery of the three intruders in his home. This could have only have been because the accused were annoyed at the meagre pickings which were the result of the burglary.

Joanne Lee Smith, whose previous convictions for violence were read out before the court, was jailed for life.

Darren Sams was ordered to be "detained during Her Majesty's pleasure" because he was a juvenile. The sentence can mean life in jail, but would be subject to review by the Home Secretary at regular intervals.

Barry John Smith, who had gone out one August night for a friendly drink with his sister-in-law and ended up instead doing a burglary and being charged with murder, was sentenced to eight years imprisonment for manslaughter.

Photograph Acknowledgements

Pen-y-Bryn Hotel, Llanfairfechan   Author's collection
Court Grange College, Newton Abbott   Author's Collection
Cafe Customers Being Questioned   South Wales Argus
Suzanne Greenhill Billboard   South Wales Argus
Timothy Robson, Snooker   Joan Robson
Suzanne Greenhill, at Newport Deaf Club   Betty Powell
Meldrum Hazell after his court case   The Scotsman
A Body Being Removed from the Cinema   Solo Syndication
Fire Officers investigating the arson attack   Solo Syndication
Tracy Turner   Leicester Mercury
Looking Down Malmesbury Road from the
killers' house   Author's Collection
Track of Bloody Footprints   Author's Collection

Research & Bibliography

1. Deaf Crime throughout the Ages - Introduction

The Forensic Status of Deaf-Mutes, Paistin Fionn (publication unknown, date circa 1910)
The Legal Status of the Deaf, Albert C.Daw, Gibson Bros. Washington, D.C. USA 1907
792 39 & 40 George III, Cap.94 (Criminal Lunatics Act, 1800)
Sutton News, 15 April 1966
Sutton Coldfield News, 24 December 1975
Rex v. Pritchard, 7 Car. & P. 304 1836
Shrewsbury Chronicle, 25 March 1836
Regina v. Whitfield, 3 Car & Kir 121 (1850)
Rex v. Governor of Stafford Prison, Ex p. Emery, 2 KB 81 (1909)
Regina v. Ragu Shan, Central Criminal Court case no. T940777 (1995)
Police and Criminal Justice Act, 1984
Briefing Paper on Deaf People and the Criminal Justice System, Bob Peckford, British Deaf Association, 1996

2. Transportation

Rex v. Steel, 1 Leach C.C.451
The Story of Betty Steel, Deaf Convict and Pioneer. Jan Branson & Don Miller, Deafness Resources Australia Ltd., Petersham, New South Wales.
Rex v. Thomas Jones, 1 Leach C.C.102
The Complete Book of Emigrants in Bondage. P.W.Coldham, Genealogical Publishing Co., Inc., Baltimore, Maryland, U.S.A.

3. The Hanged Highwayman

Chester Chronicle, 20 January 1796; 6 May 1796
Knutsford Parish Records, P7/1/4
Over Parish Records, P146/1/3; MF 157/1
Public Records Office, CHES24/179/1

4. The Drowned Baby

On the Marriage & Intermarriage of the Deaf & Dumb
Dr.D.Buxton, W.Fearnall & Co., Liverpool 1857
Glasgow Evening Mail, 11 March 1890
Edinburgh Evening Courant, 3 July 1817
Dublin Journal, 25 July 1817
Hume on Crimes, vol I, p.45
British Deaf Heritage, Peter W.Jackson, Pentland Press, Edinburgh 1990

5. An Unfortunate Pregnancy

Anecdotes and Annals of the Deaf, Dr.D.Buxton, W.Fearnall & Co., Liverpool 1854
The Sheffield Mercury, 2 October 1830
Witness Statements, Public Records Office ASSI 45/63
Indictments, Public Records Office ASSI 44/145
Parish Records, Sheffield Archives, PR 54/5
Rex v.Dyson, R.& R.C.C.523: 7 C.& P 305

6. A Christmas Affray

Birmingham Daily Post, 28 December 1875 & 3 January 1876
Birmingham Weekly Post, 15 January 1876
Witness Statements, Public Records Office ASSI 13/7

7. A Killing by Tetanus!

South Wales Daily News, 18 July 1879
South Wales Daily News, 29 & 31 May 1888
South Wales Daily News, 5 June 1888
Llandaff School for the Deaf & Dumb, Annual Report 1889

8. A Vindictive Wife

British Deaf-Mute, April 1893 (pages 87 & 96)
British Deaf-Mute, June 1893 (page 118)
British Deaf Mute, July 1893 (page 132)
Leicester Mercury, 18 February 1893, 4 July 1893

9. An Unwelcome Guest

South Wales Echo, 12,13,14,15 January 1953
South Wales Echo, 28 January 1953
South Wales Echo, 23 & 24 March 1953
Regina v. Roberts, All England Law Reports 340
Dummy, Ernest Tidyman, W.H.Allen, Publishers, London &
New York, 1974

10. Prostituted to Kill

"The Dummy", transmitted on ITV in 1989.
Bradford Telegraph & Argus, 29 & 30 August 1975
Bradford Telegraph & Argus, 21 November 1975
Bradford Telegraph & Argus, 20,21 & 22 January 1976
Personal interview, Jean Teale
Personal interviews, anonymous

11. Death at the Hands of a Client

Southern Evening Echo, 4,5 & 19 July 1978
British Deaf News, October 1978
Southern Evening Echo, 19 December 1978
Correspondence, Hampshire Constabulary Library
Correspondence, Winchester Crown Courts
Correspondence, anonymous sources.

12. The Witness Who Lied

Kilmarnock Standard, 30 October 1981
Ardrossan & Saltcoats Herald, 30 October 1981
Ardrossan & Saltcoats Herald, 6 November 1981
Kilmarnock Standard, 6 November 1981
Kilmarnock Standard, 5 February 1982
Ardrossan & Saltcoats Herald, 12 February 1982
Ardrossan & Saltcoats Herald, 19 February 1982

13. Stomped to Death

North Wales Weekly, 25 April 1985
North Wales Weekly, 14 November 1985
North Wales Weekly, 21 November 1985
North Wales Weekly, 28 November 1985
Law Reports 1990, C.L.R.123
Personal interviews, anonymous

14. A Minor Argument

British Deaf News, August 1986
Mid-Devon Advertiser, 25 April 1986; 9 May 1986
Mid-Devon Advertiser, 20 June 1986.
Mid-Devon Advertiser, 18 July 1986; 21 November 1986.

15. The Case of the Four Trials

South Wales Argus, 2, 4, 5, 11, & 12 July 1988
South Wales Argus, 3 & 6 February 1989
South Wales Argus, 18 May 1989; 3 & 4 October 1989
South Wales Argus, 1, 2, 3 & 5 February 1990
South Wales Argus, 12 July 1992
News of the World, 3 July 1988
Trial and Error Live, Channel Four Television, July 1997
British Deaf News, September 1997
One in Seven, RNID Magazine, October/November 1997
Personal interviews, anonymous sources : Gwent Constabulary
Personal interviews, anonymous people in Newport.
Personal interview, Timothy Robson
Personal interview, Joan Robson

16. Stabbed to Death

Evening Chronicle (Sunderland) 24, 28 & 29 March 1994
Personal interviews, anonymous

17. Murder by Fire

Sunderland Echo, 20 May 1993
The Journal, 20 May 1993
Sunderland Echo, 18 June 1993
Sunderland Echo, 18 & 19 July 1994; 27 July 1994
The Journal, 19 & 28 July 1994
Personal interviews, anonymous

18. A Chilling Echo of Death

Edinburgh Evening News, 6 January 1994; 27 & 28 April 1994
The Scotsman, 29 April 1994
British Deaf News, July 1994
Personal interviews, anonymous sources.

19. The Porno Cinema Fire

Today, 28 February 1994; 1, 3, 17 March 1994
Evening Standard, 28 February 1994, 1st March 1994
The Pink Paper, 4 & 11 March 1994
The Guardian, 21, 22, & 28 March 1995
The Times, 21, 25 & 28 March 1995
The British Deaf News, May 1995 issue
Personal interviews, anonymous.

20. The Last Ride

Leicestershire Mercury, 4,5,7,8,9,10,11,12 March 1994
Leicestershire Mercury, 15,16,17,18,19 March 1994
The Sun, 10 March 1994
Yes! magazine, date unknown (1997)
Personal interviews, anonymous

21. The Million Pound Mistake

Wimbledon Guardian, 4 & 11 August 1994; 1 December 1994
The Daily Telegraph, 13 June 1995; 7 October 1995
The British Deaf News, June 1995
The British Deaf News, October, November and December 1995
See Hear! magazine, October 1995
Read Hear! Teletext magazine, October 1995
Personal interviews, anonymous sources.